World Theatre in Pictures

World Theatre

from Ancient

BY

in Pictures

Times to Modern Broadway

TOM PRIDEAUX

ASSOCIATE EDITOR, LIFE MAGAZINE

Greenberg : Publisher : New York

Published in New York by Greenberg: Publisher
and simultaneously in Toronto, Canada, by Ambassador Books, Ltd.

Designer: Ernst Reichl

Library of Congress Catalog Card Number: 53-10450

Manufactured in the United States of America

To Mary Leatherbee

and the LIFE photographers

Contents

Introduction

The first reason for this book is to pay tribute to *Life's* collection of theatre photographs which has been expanding year after year since the magazine first appeared in 1936. Most of these pictures are of Broadway plays and musical shows written during the past 18 years. But in planning this book it was soon evident that the photographs added up to more than a mere 18-year slice of American theatre. They constitute a sampling of world drama from Japan to Bali to Sicily. And, moreover, because the past two decades have seen so many revivals of older plays and classic dramas, these pictures also constitute a 2000-year panorama of theatre history from Aeschylus to Broadway.

Not quite all the photographs were taken for *Life*. A few milestones in stage history are spotlighted with other photographs. But the *Life* pictures obviously steal the show. As a result, the book is too heavily weighted with modern American theatre to be balanced world history. My personal enthusiasm for particular pictures got the better of me again and again and I hadn't the strength of character to throw out handsome photographs even when they represented plays of no great historical import. There are probably too many plays by Shaw, too many musical shows, too many pictures of Bobby Clark (though not for me). I wish there had been some good picture-sequences for – to name a few–Corneille, Racine, Calderon, Goldoni, Pirandello, and Lorca. But the book, I think, still outlines enough stage history to justify its title, and I hope it will entice many readers into deeper exploration of the territory.

It has surprised some *Life* readers that a national news magazine has consistently devoted so much space to a local phenomenon like the Broadway stage. But from the beginning the planners of *Life,* led by Daniel Longwell, were aware that the New York theatre is a lively and representative part of the American scene. Other *Life* editors have also looked cordially upon the theatre. My first managing editor, John Shaw Billings, attended it rarely, but always encouraged theatre coverage, and gave it the form and direction it badly needed. His chief complaint against the theatre is the intermissions; all he really requires, I suspect, to make him a play-goer is a dinner jacket that makes him invisible.

Life's former executive editor, Wilson Hicks, was a stage enthusiast, while the present managing editor, my friend and boss, Edward K. Thompson, knows more about the theatre than I do, a fact which I try to conceal from him.

It is sometimes said that Editor-in-Chief Henry Luce dictates what his magazine shall cover in the entertainment field. This is pure nonsense. Several years ago, on one of the rare occasions when Mr. Luce, for a week or two, took over the duties of *Life's* managing editor, I wrote some complimentary words about a much-discussed drama. After reading my copy, he called me to his office and said, "I think this play is a phony." I told him I did not agree. He said, "I just wanted you to know what I think," and the original copy was printed with no changes.

Dramatic criticism in *Life,* if any, has always been brief and implied. The editors assume—rightly, I think—that the majority of readers, who seldom see the plays we cover, are interested in a straight pictorial record rather than in detailed criticism such as appears in New York newspapers. How much influence *Life* has exerted on the present state of the theatre is anybody's guess. My guess is that it is considerable, and salubrious. Certainly thousands of readers become familiar with new plays, which often turn up in community playhouses. And I like to think that the thriving condition of so many "little" theatres across the country is due in some part to *Life's* continual dissemination of theatre news.

As a rule the magazine covers only the hits, or some single element in a show which invites attention. But occasionally a life-preserver is tossed to an interesting play that has not yet caught the public's fancy. This happened with *The Madwoman of Chaillot,* and again with Menotti's opera, *The Medium,* which my colleague Gene Cook had photographed for *Life. The Medium,* after three feeble weeks, was scheduled to close on a Saturday night. On Friday the magazine story appeared. In a few hours the box-office reported an influx of business which the producer attributed directly to *Life* coverage and which encouraged him to keep his opera running another week. In a few days the theatre was crowded at every performance, and *The Medium* settled down to a profitable seance.

Ten years of covering theatre has been a continuously diverting and sometimes inspiring job, largely because of association with *Life's* group of artist-photographers. Our procedure is to look at a show, often in Boston or Philadelphia during its try-out period, and if it seems durable and interesting, to schedule a three-hour photocall on stage after an evening performance. *Life's* astute assignment editor, Ray Mackland, then books a photographer, who in turn familiarizes himself with the play.

Come the night of shooting, actors, stagehands, electricians, and other technicians are required to stand by, as pictures are taken with full scenery and properties. These midnight sessions have become a fairly regular occurrence in the Broadway theatre, and they are not always moonlight and roses. Actors, after a long ordeal of rehearsals, are apt to be tense and tired. They worry, quite understandably, about their camera angles and how much publicity they are likely to receive. One excellent actor spent most of the photocall sulking in his dressing room, and then stalked out on the stage in his underdrawers and announced that since he felt he was not being advantageously photographed he was going right home. On another occasion, a celebrated star, who is usually a teetotaler, decided to combat her weariness with a few slugs of whiskey, and cavorted hilariously through the key scenes of one of the world's greatest tragedies. Whenever the camera clicked, she jumped back into her grim role, and the pictures turned out magnificently.

Photographers are also operating under a strain. A few of them work with the normal stage lighting. Others bring their own spotlights and floodlights which must be hooked up to backstage outlets, and frantically changed and rearranged for every shot. This is the hour when people trip over wires, stagehands mutter in the wings, and tempers and fuses blow sky high. A few photographers use bulky stroboscopic units which emit an incredibly brief and intense flash (1/5,000 of a second), accompanied by a faint but sinister pop. Gjon Mili is the arch-sorcerer of the strobe units and he controls them masterfully. But strobe units have their own special demons—they sometimes refuse to function at all (which is just fine when forty dancers are going through an elaborate ballet number for you), or else, uncannily, they decide every few seconds to flash by themselves. On one interesting evening the strobes were rigged up ahead of time at an Elizabethan-style production of *Julius Caesar,* and all through the last scenes, they popped and flashed, to the profound mystification of the audience. It made a lively performance.

For all their capriciousness, however, strobe lights have been used for many of *Life's* best pictures, and on one occasion they actually helped a play in progress. Ralph Morse was assigned to shoot a religious drama in Litchfield Cathedral in England. The gracious Bishop of Litchfield requested him not to shoot during the performance. But Ralph, knowing that the success of the story depended on getting one or two shots of the audience watching the play, climbed secretly to a lofty perch and set off his strobe light at the precise instant when the actors below were enacting The Annunciation. With no disrespect intended, I must say that it gave what seemed to be a supernatural assist to the Immaculate Conception, and the audience thought it was part of the play. As it happened, that particular picture failed to turn out, which probably was divine vengeance.

To *Life* photographers goes the credit for having developed a new style of theatre photography, in contrast to the usual frozen stills which are customary for lobby displays and newspaper reproduction. Their aim is to create a candid-picture sequence which catches the play in action (whole scenes are reenacted for the cameraman), and at the same time to enhance the mood of the play by special lighting and composition. Each photographer stamps his work with a more or less individual style. Eileen Darby's work has special clarity and to-the-pointness; George Karger's has humor and inventiveness; Eugene Smith carries his deep feeling for humanity into the theatre and is equally skillful with *Death of a Salesman* or *South Pacific;* Phillippe Halsman's pictures have a richness and sensuality that illumines a Dostoievskian tragedy or a line of chorus beauties; Eliot Elisofon has a sharp dramatic sense for such plays as *Native Son* and *A Streetcar Named Desire;* and Eric Schaal's touch is always sensitive and keen. Gjon Mili, over a longer span of time than any other photographer, has given *Life,* I think, its most distinctive theatre coverage; his pictures alone would make a brilliant album. And there are many others who have had fewer Broadway assignments, but whose work has much excellence.

Hand in hand with the photographers have been many *Life* staff members (Timothy Foote, Philip Kunhardt, Robert Ginna, Laura Ecker) who have originated picture ideas and gone forth at midnight to serve as trouble shooters and guiding spirits. Outstanding among them all is Mary Leatherbee—she is now *Life's* Motion Picture Editor —whose artistry, energy, and tact have helped create many of the best pictures in this book. Working with her for 8 years has been a joy.

In the rush to prepare this volume against a deadline, many friends have helped. Robert Campbell wrote the inspiring introduction to Greek drama. Robert Wallace let me use his amusing paragraph, first printed in *Life,* under the picture of Jimmy Durante and squirrel. Rolla Prideaux gave me the benefit of her wit and learning in theatre history. Gene Cook, Maitland Edey, Timothy Foote, Joseph Kastner and Robert Wernick helped with short bits of text. The people in *Life's* Picture Collection and Photographic Laboratory were exceedingly generous. A bibliography is printed at the end of the book, but I acknowledge a special debt to *A History of the Theatre* by Freedley and Reeves, which I plundered freely. In closing, I can't say enough in praise of Doris O'Neil , who stood by through this whole operation, and raised efficiency from a virtue to an art.

The Way It Began

"I go to the theatre to be entertained," is a statement often spoken nowadays, usually in protest against thought-provoking plays. Certainly, one function of the stage is to provide pure enjoyment—the more, the better. But to ask the theatre to serve no other purpose is to misunderstand its true character and potentialities, its breadth and greatness, and, to the point here, its origin.

Quite literally, the theatre begins in the sun and stars. For it is the Earth, spinning on its tilted axis and, in turn, spinning around the sun, which produced the first drama—the cycle of seasons: death in winter, rebirth in spring. It is hard to imagine any drama on the planet Venus, which always keeps one side to the sun and has no seasons, no progression of moods, no climaxes. On Earth primitive man was deeply moved by this seasonal spectacle; it involved his urge to live and his practical struggle for existence.

Practicality is the keynote of all early theatre, which is inextricably bound up with early religion, and which took the form of propitiatory rites. Nobody went to the theatre, so to speak, to be entertained. They went to get something done, to petition for more sun, more rain, more fish in the sea, more game on the land, to be made fertile, victorious, healthy, holy and immortal, to incur the favor of powerful gods and quash the malignant ones, to increase their courage and ease their sorrows. They went in order to go on living.

The word *drama* derives from the Greek *dromenon*, "a thing done." In ancient Greece, the most impressive thing done, ritually speaking, was the spring ceremony of Dionysus, the god of vegetation, fruitfulness, death and rebirth. Dionysus was the son of Zeus, the fertilizing god of rain, and Semele, a personification of Earth. When Semele was killed by lightning, her infant child, Dionysus, was saved from the surrounding flames by Zeus, who enclosed him in his own thigh until he reached maturity and then brought him to light. Thus Dionysus was twice-born. Variations on the legend are numerous, but the salient fact is that Dionysus was resurrected. This miracle, so profoundly important to the human spirit, was celebrated by the entire population, which indeed caused it to take place. Dionysus was personified by a youth, who became the god himself, surrounded by a band of followers who danced and chanted in his honor.

As Greek civilization advanced, the ceremony became a kind of rustic rite, which most people watched from the sidelines. About the year 527 B.C. the Athenian ruler Pisistratus decreed that the festival should be amplified by enactments of heroic tales of Homer. These dramatizations, beginning as story-telling accompanied by choral chants, were performed on the ground sacred to Dionysus outside of Athens.

Tiers of seats in a vast semicircle were constructed on the hillside, and the actors were confined to a small area known as the *skenè*. The dancing place, or doing place, virtually disappeared, and was superceded by the spectator place. This change of architecture on the Athenian hillside indicated a change of architecture in the human mind. From being an active participant in the theatre, man was becomng an observer, a contemplator. He was preparing himself for more thoughtfulness, reflection, introspection, and vicarious emotion, for the genius of Sophocles and Shakespeare, for the ills and glories of the future.

American Indian

Dance dramas are a vital element in the life of the American Indian. He dances as a warrior, acting out his tracking of the enemy, the struggle, and his own victory. He dances the Sun Dance which insures good hunting and keeps the world in order. He dances to insure good corn, and to deliver the Indian from the white man. During the ceremonies, the dancers are believed actually to become the gods they represent. Rituals are dangerous as well as beneficial because the dancer or priest can easily make a misstep or minor error which will bring the opposite of what he desires.

A Fire Dance marks the coming of age of an Apache girl. The ceremony represents the creation of earth and man, and carries the girl symbolically through her life into happy old age. Here the she-mountain Gods wear fantastic headdresses and carry yucca swords to drive away all evil disease-producing spirits.

This New Mexican Indian wears a headdress of evergreens and antlers in order to perform the Deer Dance, which will enable him to hunt and shoot the deer, his most important source of meat.

A group of South African gold miners (left) perform their tribal dances on holidays and weekends, while their compatriots watch from a hillside.

Africa

The pantomime dance is Africa's major dramatic form. And in many instances the other arts — music, self-adornment, and the decoration of ritual objects — evolved to supplement the great story-telling dances. The African acts out in dance everything that is important to him: his love of living, his fear of dying. His dances can be rigidly formal, as in the stylizations of human sacrifice, or wildly grotesque, as in the hate dances. But they are always strongly dramatic, strongly rhythmic, crucially related to life itself.

A Shilluk warrior of the Upper Nile contorts his face and body in a violent war dance. Performed by one man, it represents a fierce but graceful battle against a powerful unseen adversary.

Some of the best dancers among the South African miners perform their tribal rites with torsos and legs draped with sheep wool.

Brandishing spears and shields, a leopard-decorated Zulu leads his tribesmen in a ceremonial dance of the Natal region.

A Balinese myth comes to life as a heroic lion (center) fights off a Witch Queen (rear) to the delight of a clown (foreground).

Bali

Ritual drama reached a high point of perfection in the story-telling dances of Bali. From infancy certain Balinese children are singled out to be temple dancers, and taught a whole, unique vocabulary of dance movements—movements that suggest the fantastic birds, flowers, and even the architecture of Bali. In 1952 a troupe of 16 dancers and 23 musicians left their lovely island homeland for the first time and made a triumphant visit to London and the U. S. Their dances, rooted in Balinese folklore, abounded with monsters, demons, clowns, hunters, lovers.

Bali's star male dancer imitates a he-bee trying to woo a she-bee (left) who is more interested in flitting than flirting.

Carrying on the ancient ritualistic custom of mimicking animals, these Balinese males perform a weird chant imitating an army of growling, hissing monkeys.

**Atremble with her evil news,
12-year-old Ni Gusta Raka
as a bird of death stands poised
to bring prophecy of doom to a king.**

Haiti

The annual Mardi Gras among the high-spirited and talented natives of Haiti is a contemporary expression of the Dionysian impulse for a springtime revel. The whole community participates, acting out folktales, proverbs, and mystical rites, and impersonating beasts, birds, and fantastic hybrids like the feathered hogs' heads worn by the two revelers below.

The Glory that Was Greece

There are two brief moments in the history of the Western World which will forever bear the mark of the miraculous; eras so inspired that they transcend history and the affairs of men and exist, instead, on a more permanent plane—reflecting eternity. Explanation in terms of social organization, commerce, economics, and ideology fades to an inaudible uncertainty beside the achievements themselves. For these were the times when civilization, like Moses, ascended a shrouded mountain and in that journey a past perished and a future was prescribed. During each pilgrimage civilization died, and man returned again to live in a new world, severed irrevocably from the old.

One pilgrimage took place in the Middle Ages, which left as their imperishable monuments the great cathedrals. Constructed by patient men, stone upon stone, they embody design that is not mortal. The towers of the cathedral at Chartres or the vaults of Notre Dame reflect a purity of inspiration that mortal man does not know. For these lovely things were the work of God. And though men built them, yet stone does not make a living Chartres or a Notre Dame. They stand instead as signs that the spirit of faith was breathed into the spirit of man and that at one point in history a spark, which long ago burst forth so precariously, burned bright enough to inflame a whole civilization.

Some sixteen centuries before the Middle Ages the other miraculous moment occurred. Along the bright shores of the Aegean Sea, in the little world of Greece, man first discovered the spirit of man. With that discovery the Western World was born, as well as that many-faceted mirror of human life—the theatre. Nearly everything the Greeks did was great, and all of it was glorious. The Greek drama is no exception. Of the four great writers of tragedy three are Greek and the fourth is Shakespeare. Only a gifted people and an incredible convergence of circumstances could have brought forth tragedy, full-blown, from the head of Athena.

The Greeks inherited a world of myth and superstition, a world in which nature was a magical puppet show and the puppeteers devils and demons. To man the purposes of nature were inscrutable, often malignant, and ever dominated by the wakeful eye of treachery. Nature was to be placated by magic rather than used by intelligence, for man was a ritualistic rather than a rational animal.

This was the primitive world, and the Greeks hated it passionately. The Greeks loved life, hoped for happiness, feared death, flocked to the theatre, enjoyed games and discourse and drinking. The first realists, they regarded the world as something to be understood and they faced it unflinchingly. In their ceaseless pursuit of truth the Greeks turned mankind upside down or rather, for the first time, right side up, elevating intelligence. With that act man became a creature who could reason, understand, and wonder. This achievement alone would have made the Greeks memorable, but it is what followed that made them miraculous.

For once they discovered that life was good and the world intelligible, the Greeks pressed relentlessly along every path of inquiry. In astronomy they were the first to explain the motions of the stars and planets and to discover the earth was round. Detesting the despotism of the East, they invented democracy, established its basic laws, and pursued it vehemently. The Greeks wrote the first history, and no historian surpasses the Athenian Thucydides. What building stands in the world today more beautiful than the Parthenon at Athens, unless it be Chartres?

But it is in philosophy and tragedy that the Greek world is supreme. So elevated are the works of Plato and Aristotle that a modern philosopher has said that all the books since have added little more than footnotes to those great men; so noble the tragedies that over and over again their characters glide spectre-like through the little Globe theatre of Shakespeare. How like Macbeth sounds Orestes, who has just killed his mother because she murdered his father:

ORESTES: Did she do it or did she not? The proofs you know—the deed and the death. I am victor but vile, polluted.

CHORUS: One trouble is here—another comes.

ORESTES: Hear me and learn, for I know not how it will end, I am borne along by a runaway horse. My thoughts are out of bounds. Fear leaps at my heart. Before my reason goes—oh, you my friends, I say I killed my mother—yet not without reason—she was vile and she killed my father and God hated her. Look — Look — Women — there — there — Black — all black, and long hair twisting like snakes. Oh let me go.

CHORUS: What fancies trouble you, O son, faithful to your father? Do not fear.

ORESTES: No fancies. My mother has sent them. They throng upon me and from their eyes blood drips, blood of hate. You see them not? I — I see them. They drive me. I cannot stay.

And how like King Lear is Oedipus the King, who has blinded himself and is going into exile, leaving the throne to his friend Creon. He asks that Creon bring his daughters to him:

OEDIPUS: If it is lawful, let me touch them with my hands. Grant it, Prince, grant it, noble heart. I would believe, could I touch them, that I still saw them. But do I hear them sobbing? Has Creon pitied me and sent my children, my darlings? Has he done this?

What thoughts lie more in the main stream of human emotions than these—a father's love of his children; a man's fear of his own acts? Greek drama was born in mid-stream because it rose from a far older stream—primitive ritual. In primitive Athens there was a great spring festival for the god Dionysus, the god who brought fertility to the fields. The festival was accompanied by ceremonies and sacrifices in which a handsome youth, surrounded by a chorus of singers and dancers, represented the god. By the 6th century B.C. many Athenians had grown too subtle to believe in the fallible gods of Homer. They eliminated Dionysus from the spring festival and substituted instead reënactments of the heroic tales every Greek knew by heart—the stories of Agamemnon at Troy, of Prometheus, of the Seven Against Thebes. The handsome youth became the hero, and the chorus the commentator on the hero's actions. The poets of Athens were called upon to dramatize the stories, and because the stories were of epic dimensions the birth of an exalted tragedy was possible.

It was born under remarkably auspicious circumstances. With candor and simplicity the Greek mind was struggling with the fundamental problems of human life. The gods were cast down, and everywhere the Greeks were searching for a less perishable reality. This was a new enterprise for man and a vastly exciting one, for the goal was the crystal air of Olympus which had never been breathed before. Because this was the first ascent of the mountain of the mind it had a directness, honesty, and unconscious purity about it that can never be recaptured. Simplicity is characteristic of the whole of Greek writing, drawn as it was for an audience vibrant with the experience of the pilgrimage. Men of later ages, satiated with lush descriptions of the flora and fauna of the mountain of reason, have returned instinctively to that ancient homeland for a purity of perception found only in the literature of Greece.

The Greeks did not try to wring all the overtones from an idea with multitudinous words. Instead they stated the idea with a simplicity that has an astonishing dramatic effect; and such was their genius for finding the touchstone of an idea that more meaning echoes in the corridors of the mind than could ever be suggested by words. At the battle of Thermopylae a handful of Spartans fought to the last man, holding the pass for days against the host of Persia. That action saved Greece, and the Greeks erected a plaque afterward to commemorate their heroism. The simple inscription read: "Stranger, go tell Sparta that we lie here in obedience to her laws." There is no long eulogy, no flow of words. Words cannot contain the meaning of such an event. But a simple statement, beautifully and truly written, can evoke in the mind of the stranger a moving image of what happened at Thermopylae. For nothing is so dramatic as the real and turning world of life, and the great writer is not one who would make a world out of words, but a man who tries to find words for the world.

The writers of Greek tragedy—Aeschylus, Sophocles, and Euripides—reflect this feeling intensely. In a few brief sentences they can evoke a complete and deeply human character, simply because the words chosen tap areas in every man's experience which are already rich in imagery and emotion. Thus the drama unfolding on the stage evokes a far richer drama from the well of human experience.

A third drama is evoked on a level completely above the play. The mind of Greece, probing everywhere with its delight in reason, might have concluded that reason was the master of all things. But such was the Greek genius that it reached the opposite answer. Above Sophocles' *Oedipus the King* a host of questions drift: questions of predestination, of free will, of how the man who is righteous can bring about a calamity of evil, why he should be punished, whether he can be forgiven. In *Antigone* the laws of the state decree that the heroine cannot bury her brother honorably, but she appeals to a divine law above the laws of men and dies for her belief in it. In the *Agamemnon* sins pass from generation to generation and are resolved only by divine sanction.

Through its love of reason the Greek mind found divinity far beyond the gods of Homer and far above the mind itself. Confronted with the ultimate and unanswerable questions, Socrates, the noblest of all, said that only his guardian angel could tell him which was right or wrong. This sense of the inexplicable was the final miracle of Greece. In Athens there was an altar which bore the inscription: "To the Unknown God." This was the god Athens finally perceived, and with that perception came a sense of humility and human warmth. In his last speech to the court which has condemned him unjustly Socrates forgives the jury and says: "Now we must part, you to live and I to die. Which is better, only God knows." And in *Oedipus at Colonus*, the sequel and final answer to the story of Oedipus, Sophocles presents a transformed hero. After 20 years of blind wandering, led by his daughter, Oedipus enters to open the play:

OEDIPUS: My daughter—daughter of the blind old man—
Where, I wonder, have we come to now?
What place is this, Antigone? What people?
Who will be kind to Oedipus this evening
And give the wanderer charity?
Though he ask little and receive less,
It is sufficient,
    Suffering and time,
Vast time, have been instructors in contentment . . .

At the end of the play, as he is about to die, Oedipus speaks to his daughters:

OEDIPUS: Children, this day your father is gone from you.
All that was mine is gone. You shall no longer
Bear the burden of taking care of me—
I know it was hard, my children. And yet one word
Makes all those difficulties disappear:
That word is *love* . . .

With the passing of Socrates and Sophocles the stage of Greece was left bare, waiting for the day when the unknown god would be made known by Christianity.

The Persians

One of the first plays by the father of Greek drama, *The Persians* deals compassionately with the enemy's defeat at Salamis, and stands as a noble landmark in the brief history of man's humanity to man. Aeschylus knew whereof he wrote, for he fought the Persians at Marathon and was probably at Salamis when their fleet went down. His tragedy offers little action, but in his eloquent dialogue we behold "the sea with foul wrecks and blood disfigured," and see the defeated King Xerxes among "the feeble few" who "dragged on their toilsome march to reach their native soil."

The messenger is a central figure in all Greek tragedies. Tradition seldom permits scenes of horror and bloodshed to be performed on stage, so it is the messenger's role to describe these disasters. In *The Persians*, the messenger (Vittorio Gassman) comes to the palace of the conquered Persian king at Susa and shouts, "Woe to the towns through Asia's peopled realms!" Then after a bitter report, he ends with, "But many of the ills that burst upon us I refrain to utter."

The messenger recounts the calamity to Atossa, mother of the defeated King Xerxes. The spirit of Aeschylus stands beside her, too noble to gloat over a fallen enemy.

In 1950 *The Persians* was given by a group of Italian actors in one of the same theatres near Syracuse, Sicily, where it was shown some 2400 years ago.

Sophocles: Oedipus

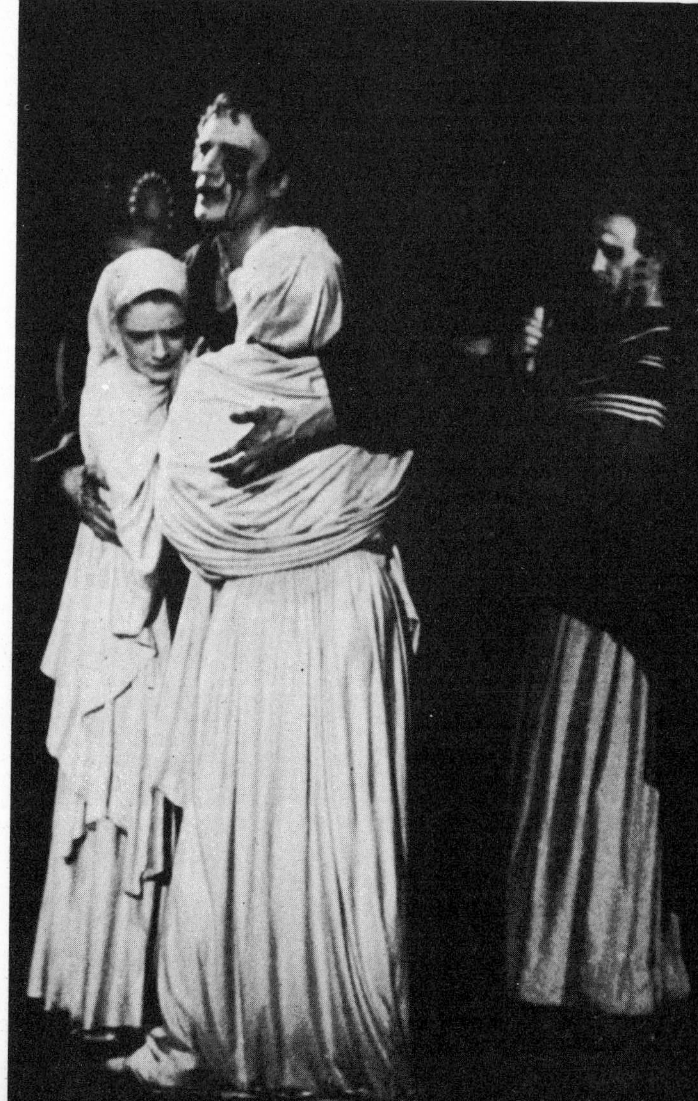

This great tragedy by the great Sophocles, who "saw life steadily and saw it whole," tells of Oedipus who unwittingly killed his father, Laius, and married his mother—murder and incest committed in complete innocence.

In the beginning, when the Oracle warned King Laius that some day he would be slain by his son, the Queen, Jocasta, left her infant in the wilds to die. He was found, grew up in faraway Corinth, and while travelling killed a stranger—named Laius.

Before King Oedipus' palace (left) the blind seer Teiresias (center) at first refuses to speak. The King goads him until the seer cries, "The killer you are seeking is yourself."

Oedipus (Sir Laurence Olivier) hears his subjects beg for deliverance from a deadly and mysterious plague. Word arrives from the oracle of Apollo that the plague will end if the slayer of King Laius, who was killed years ago, is finally punished.

In his final agony, Oedipus untied the rope with which his mother-wife hanged herself, took the golden pins from her robe, and plucked out his eyeballs. Blind, he clings to his daughters, one of whom is the doomed Antigone.

Medea, alone, gloats over her vengeful
plot to slay Jason's bride by sending
her a crown and robe dipped in deadly venom.

King Creon, Creusa's father, orders
Medea to take her two little sons into exile.
Her barbarian magic might prove deadly.

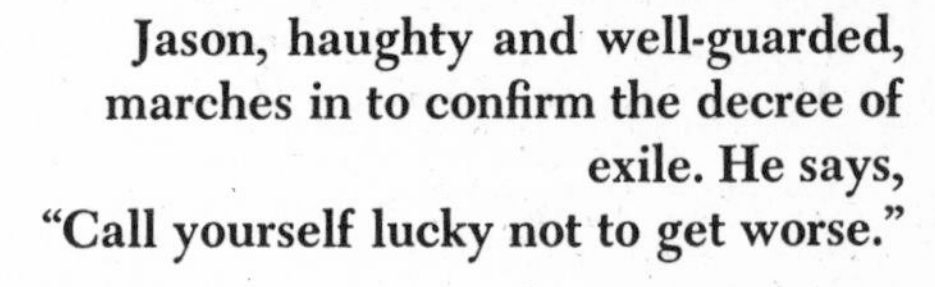

Jason, haughty and well-guarded,
marches in to confirm the decree of
exile. He says,
"Call yourself lucky not to get worse."

Jason and his sons, believing Medea has
softened, set out with her gift
which will bring agonizing death to
Creusa and Creon.

Euripides: Medea

Robinson Jeffers adapted Euripides' tragedy for Judith Anderson, who made a fiery and lethal Medea. John Gielgud was the self-obsessed Jason, who docked the Argo at Colchis to steal the Golden Fleece. There he won the king's daughter, Medea, whose "rapid and tricky wisdom" got him the fleece and swept many dangers from his path. After years of marriage, Jason cast Medea aside to wed Creusa; not as he says "out of blind passion . . . but to achieve power."

Medea's handmaidens are appalled at her fury. One cries, "My heart is a shaken cup of terror."

Medea (continued)

As her last vengeful act against Jason, the demoniacal Medea slaughters their two beloved children and bids him gaze upon her bloody deed.

Sophocles: Electra

The brooding Electra lives in the house of her sinful mother, Clytemnestra, who years ago conspired with her lover, Aegisthus, to slay her husband, Agamemnon. Her son, Orestes, fled from his mother, but Electra, cruelly treated, stays on with the guilty pair. Electra's only love is for her dead father and vanished brother. Orestes finally returns to avenge his father's death, but to take the slayers unaware, he sends his old tutor ahead with word of his death. Electra's plunge into despair, and her final joy, make one of the most moving climaxes in Greek drama.

Orestes, seeing Electra's grief as she clasps the urn which she thinks holds his ashes, says, "What words can serve me in this pass!"

Electra, wild with joy when she learns that the stranger is her brother, throws herself at the tutor's feet, crying, "O messenger whose feet were kindly servants! Hail Father!"

Lonely and desperate, Electra dreams only of seeing her beloved brother. Katina Paxinou and Thanos Kotsopoulos of the National Theatre of Greece gave a memorable performance of this tragedy on Broadway in 1952—with special honors going to a superbly trained chorus.

Narrator, representing Greek chorus, points out the characters. Antigone (Katharine Cornell) sits alone at rear. Standing are her sister and lover.

Antigone was impressively modernized by Jean Anouilh to hearten France during the Nazi occupation, though some of its Sophoclean force was lost because attacks on dictatorship had to be veiled. During the year it ran in Paris the Germans did not see themselves embodied in King Creon, nor the French in the heroic girl Antigone.

This deep and simple tragedy centers around Antigone's efforts to bury her brother, who was slain in a battle for the throne. King Creon, for reasons of State, decrees that the corpse be left to rot unburied, which to the Greeks was a ghastly crime. In 1946 a distinguished American production had Katharine Cornell as Antigone, who finally dies trying to honor her brother.

Haemon, Creon's son, is one of the theatre's great lovers. In the end he kills himself so his soul can join Antigone.

Sophocles:

Antigone

Ismene begs her sister not to risk her young life for their dead brother. But Antigone's love is stronger than her fear.

Antigone (continued)

Sir Cedric Hardwicke was a flawlessly suave, steel-trap Creon. But the steel buckles when he finds he has driven his own son to death.

Antigone, seized while burying her brother, is dragged before Creon. Though she fails in her mission and dies tragically, her dauntless and loving spirit is the final victor.

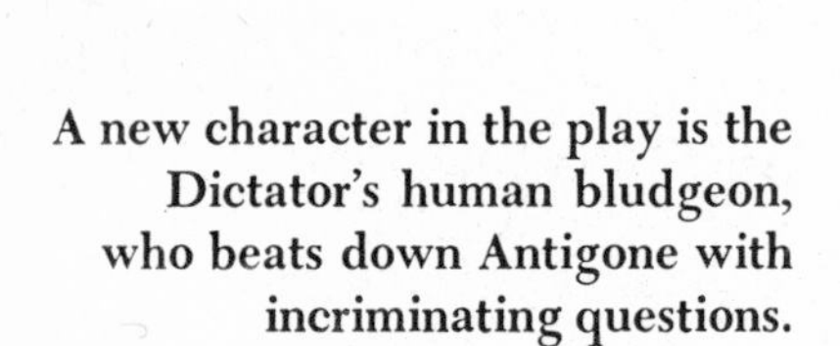

A new character in the play is the Dictator's human bludgeon, who beats down Antigone with incriminating questions.

Euripides: Bacchi

The evil spell wears off. Agave cries, "The head— O God—of Pentheus. How come I to hold this thing?"

38 While revelling bewitched with the Bacchi, Agave, thinking her son Pentheus is a lion, cuts off his head and proudly shows it to her father Cadmus.

Euripides' tragedy *The Bacchi* tells the story of King Pentheus who is bent on stamping out the orgiastic cult of the wine-god Dionysus. Enraged, the god himself appears as a handsome young visitor and wields his power over the King's mother, Agave.

When Dionysus pleads, "Peace, musical sisters, I'm covered with blisters," the frogs say, "Co-ax, co-ax."

Aristophanes: the Frogs

The fearless wit and Olympian slapstick of Aristophanes—the father of all comedy—is seldom seen now outside of university productions. *The Frogs* seems to be especially in favor because it lends itself to swimming-pool high jinks. It deals with a journey taken by Dionysus, god of drama, to Hades where he attends a contest between Aeschylus and Euripides to determine who writes greater tragedy. Aeschylus wins.

Hercules (left) is upset when a stranger calls, disguised as himself. It is just Dionysus asking the way to Hades.

Charon, the ferryman to Hades, makes poor Dionysus row to the rhythmical croaking of the frogs

When Dionysus cries, "Would you have me row till my shoulder cracks?" Yale University's frogs sing, "Brekekekex co-ax, co-ax."

Aristophanes: The Birds

In a production by the Yale Dramatic Association, the poet descends from the balcony. After hearing his silly verses (below), the birds bounce him in a blanket.

In this boisterous comedy, Euelpides and Pithetaerus leave Athens to escape the burdens of civilization. They come to the kingdom of The Birds, and at once urge them to build a city—Cloud Cuckoo Land—which they do with magical speed: 30,000 cranes bring stones, 10,000 storks make bricks. No-good people begin to troop in: an oracle-monger, a shifty informer, a piffling poet. But out they go. The Birds get so powerful that Zeus makes a peace pact with them and gives Pithetaerus his lovely lightning-maker, Basileia, for a wife.

Cloud Cuckoo Land celebrates the nuptials of Pithetaerus and Basileia.

And the Comedy that Was Rome

The Roman theatre stemmed from the clowning and bald jesting of folk festivals, combined with music and dancing imported down the coast from Etruria. The lovely Trinclinio tomb paintings testify to the grace and snap of these dances, and the folk festivals have been compared to Edwardian English music hall shows.

The first Roman theatres were temporary wooden scaffoldings erected on the street, with only a painted backdrop for scenery. It depicted two or three houses in front of which all action took place: domestic spats, lovers' meetings, sly skulduggery. These drops were similar to the gaudy street scenes that used to be a horror and a delight in every U.S. vaudeville theatre. Some spectators sat in jerry-built bleachers; the rest stood around. Everybody drifted up—citizens, slaves, housewives, hussies.

The first Roman play with a real plot was translated by Livius Andronicus from the Greek in 240 B.C. From then on, as part of Rome's colossal cribbing of Greek culture, Roman drama consisted largely of translations or adaptations from the Greek. But Romans had their own genius for comedy, and the genius of Roman comedy was Plautus (c.254 B.C. – c.184 B.C.). Plautus' comedies abound with slick plots, cases of mistaken identity, girl-and-boy mixups of astonishing variety, puns and jokes.

Rome's other great writer of comedy, Terence, took his plays openly from the Greek masters, Menander and Apollodorus. Terence wrote with more polish, drew character and built plots more carefully than Plautus did. But Plautus was better theatre.

Some censorship was imposed. Public and political figures could not be criticized. It was safe to rib the skirt-chasing of Jupiter, but no digs at Fabius Maximus. This, of course, differed totally from the Greek point of view, which permitted Aristophanes to rib all the public and political figures he had a mind to. Roman comedy at its best is shrewd, human, intimate, and impudent. But its best is too infrequent. Rome's foolish censorship of the stage left us a heritage of triviality.

It was not until 55 B.C. that the first great stone amphitheatre was built. Then huge stadiums went up throughout the Empire. No admissions were charged, but numbered tickets were issued. The drop curtain was used, behind which were erected elaborate scenes with wooden roofs built over the stage to protect them. As the spectacles became more magnificent, the plays grew more trivial. Agamemnon made his entrance in *Clytemnestra* accompanied by six hundred pack mules.

Seneca (4 B.C.–A.D. 65), last of the great dramatists, wrote only tragedies. We have no evidence that any of his plays were produced in Rome, but they were read and greatly admired in private circles. He gloried in scenes of gruesome violence which the wise Greeks allowed to occur only off-stage. Replete with high-flown phrases, Seneca's works have "a wearisome display of learning." During the Renaissance, however, he became so popular that his plays were not only acted, but widely copied. No other classical dramatist had as much influence as did Seneca in the 16th, 17th, and 18th centuries. But while Seneca finally had his reign, Plautus has reigned longer through his influence upon Molière, Shakespeare, and Ben Jonson, and upon the comedy of today.

The Roman theatre first played in the streets, then went crazy in the Colosseum, and at last crawled into the closet where it smothered.

The Merchant

This lively street scene, typical of most Roman comedies, was designed by Broadway's gifted Donald Oenslager for a Yale Drama School production. Plautus in *The Merchant* unfolds a raffish plot about a young man sailing in from Rhodes with a pretty young mistress. His doddering father kidnaps her for his own pleasure but dares not take her home lest his wife get testy. A neighbor, whose wife is away, is happy to oblige by giving the girl shelter. When the neighbor's wife returns unexpectedly, there is a good deal of yelping and fist-shaking on the sidewalk. In the end the father backs out of the picture and the son moves in.

Jean Louis Barrault as Mercury is the henchman of Jupiter. Perched on a cloud, Mercury aids the great god in his amorous exploits by summoning darkness, which arrives in the form of the Queen of the Night drawn by two horses.

Moliere's Amphitryon

Plautus is seldom performed nowadays. But since the plot of his excellent *Amphitryon* bobs up again and again, three later versions of it are shown here in Plautus' honor. The ancient story tells how the god Jupiter set out to woo a mortal beauty, Alcmene, by disguising himself as her husband, Amphitryon. Moliere's version was brought to the U.S. in 1952 by the Jean Louis Barrault repertory.

A closer view of the Queen of the Night shows her to be a pretty French actress.

Amphitryon 38

From the modern French version by Jean Giraudoux—he arbitrarily called it *Amphitryon 38* because it is at least the 38th retelling—the American playwright S. N. Behrman made a brilliant adaptation. It was given on Broadway with Alfred Lunt and Lynn Fontanne as Jupiter and Alcmene, and a handsome Theatre Guild production designed by Lee Simonson.

In the play's prologue, Jupiter and his henchman Mercury (Richard Whorf) rest their plaster bodies on a cloud, while Jupiter peers down on earth and falls madly in love with a warrior's wife, Alcmene.

A happily married woman, Alcmene accepts the admiration of the great god Jupiter, but never dreams of betraying her husband.

Now that crafty Jupiter has assumed the guise of her husband Amphitryon, Alcmene has the unique honor of darning a god's socks.

Out of This World, a 1950 Broadway musical version of the Amphitryon story, with songs by Cole Porter, would have amazed and probably pleased Plautus. Billy Redfield was Mercury, and a Negro dancer, Janet Collins, made an exciting Queen of the Night.

Out of this World

The Theatre Goes to Church

Again and again in the history of civilization, Church and Theatre have gone hand in hand. Ancient Egypt had its religious spectacle depicting the death and resurrection of Osiris. Greece had its early Dionysian rites which gave rise to the first great age of dramatic literature. Primitive people the world over have channeled their religious impulse into all manner of dramatic presentations. So it is not surprising to find that Christianity during its flowering in the Middle Ages also turned to the theatre. To be sure, after the licentiousness of the late Roman stage, the Church for many centuries had denounced the theatre as if it were a disreputable cousin. But in the very nature of things the cousins belong together, so in the 9th century the Church began putting on what were called Mysteries or Miracles.

One of the first productions was a simple enactment of Good Friday, showing the arrival of the three Marys at Christ's tomb where they see an angel holding a palm. About the year 1000 a nun, Hrosvitha, wrote six plays, modeled on the comedies of Terence (expurgated, of course).

Before long the staging of Ecclesiastical Drama became more and more spectacular. Tempests, earthquakes, and mysterious disappearances were featured. Settings depicting Hell were hugely enjoyed by medieval audiences. Mechanical jaws opening while hairy devils with pitchforks drove shrieking victims into the flames made a bigger hit than halos, harps, and caroling angels.

Usually these pageants were given in the porticos of cathedrals; some were held in the Coliseum at Rome. The lists of costumes and properties are interesting. We read: "2 cotes and a payre hosen for Eve, stayned. A cote wt hosen and tayle for ye serpente. And among expense accounts: "A rope for Judas, 2 d; a girdle for God, 3 d [*d* means *penny*]."

Some festivals were comic or even bawdy. Coming after solemn church rituals, they must have served to relieve emotional tension in much the same way as the Satyr plays which used to follow the Greek tragedies. For example, there were The Feast of the Ass, suggested by Balaam's donkey or the entry into Jerusalem, and the Feast of the Fools led by the Pope of Fools, in which participants wore bizarre costumes or none at all. Just about everything was dramatized from *The Beginning of the World* to the *Massacre of the Innocents*. The merchant and craftsmen's Guilds took a hand in spectacles suited to their professions. Cooks put on *The Harrowing of Hell;* shipwrights did *The Building of the Ark;* fishmongers, *The Flood*. When the secular theatre began to play a return engagement in the 1400's the Church had kept the footlights burning.

Today the most famous Miracle Play still being performed is at Oberammergau. The Morality Play *Everyman* remains a perennial favorite at schools and churches, and recently was produced beautifully at Salzburg.

For this book there are no photographs of historical Church plays, except *Everyman*. Three modern plays are included, however, because they have been performed in church settings, and preserve, to some degree, the spirit of the Mysteries.

After the repentant airman has carried alone the cross of Christ, his redeemed spirit watches the Persona Dei crown Mary.

England's magnificent Litchfield Cathedral was the scene of this modern Mystery given in 1946. In a final tableau the Persona Dei, or Christ, stands before the Cross of Glory.

The Just Vengeance

This morality play by Dorothy Sayers follows the old Church dramas by having such Biblical characters as Adam, Eve, Cain, Abel, and the Recording Angel, as well as the citizens of Litchfield and a British airman. The airman, shot down on a wartime mission, stumbles up the church aisle and sees the living truths of the Bible enacted before his eyes. Skeptical at first, his soul finds salvation in the love and wisdom of Christ.

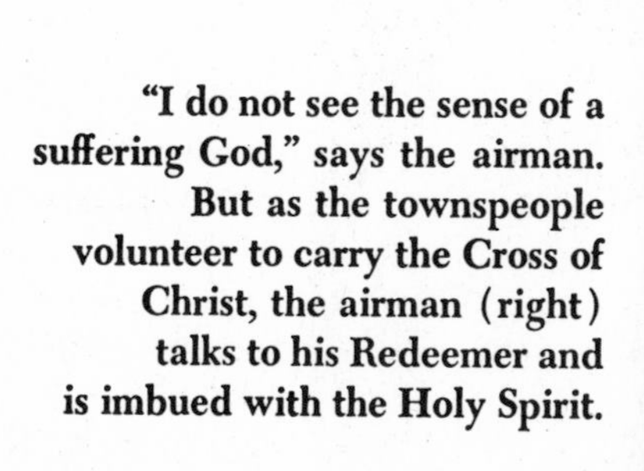

"I do not see the sense of a suffering God," says the airman. But as the townspeople volunteer to carry the Cross of Christ, the airman (right) talks to his Redeemer and is imbued with the Holy Spirit.

The play opens as a herald announces that Thomas has returned from France. The priests' joy at his sudden homecoming is mixed with fear of a conflict between him and the King.

The Tempter gives Thomas a picture of his hidden ambition: martyrdom. He tells him he can increase his power by making himself "lowest on earth, to be high in heaven."

Murder in the Cathedral, a verse drama written by T. S. Eliot in 1935, is set in Canterbury Cathedral where Archbishop Thomas à Becket was killed by a band of knights in 1170. But it wasn't until 1939 when these pictures were taken in the chapel of Hobart College, Geneva, New York, that the play was first performed in church. The play tells of Thomas's uncertainty as to what he will do next in a feud he has had with King Henry II about royal encroachments on the church. Four tempters offer him first obvious worldly temptations, then the subtle appeal of a martyr's death as a dramatic climax to his stormy career. Choosing this last, Thomas becomes St. Thomas by giving himself into the hands of his assassins.

At the altar where his priests had led him for safety, Thomas à Becket is slaughtered by knights who believe that England could best be served by his death. Thomas had fought for the church against royal encroachments.

Choruses in the play are chanted by girls behind a transparent screen representing a stained glass window.

Murder in the Cathedral

Thomas is dead 28 days after his return. Here the play ends. In history, Henry II, who deplored the act of his overzealous courtiers, did public penance for Thomas' death.

A Sleep of Prisoners

Christopher Fry's modern poetic drama, which opened in New York's St. James Church in 1951 after a London success, is directly descended from medieval morality plays. It concerns four war prisoners hiding in an enemy church. Each has dreams based on Bible legends, in which all the prisoners take part, and which illustrate not only each prisoner's own thoughts and tensions but also those of all contemporary men. At the end the fourth prisoner, Pvt. Meadows, speaks the play's best lines when, counseling his companions against despair, he challenges them to "Thank God our time is now, when wrong comes up to face us everywhere . . ."

The prisoners fill their mattresses before turning in. Behind them are two bunks backed by an ornate altar screen. Here Pvt. Meadows (lower right) tells how he got into the army.

In a dream scene Abraham (Pvt. King) tries to find the courage to sacrifice his beloved son Isaac (Pvt. Able) to Almighty God.

Shadrac, Meshac, Abednego, are enacted in the dreams by three soldiers. Thrust into a fiery furnace, they find that only loyalty to each other can save them from destruction.

Everyman

Edith Wynne Matthison, in her famous production of the play, was Everyman. After a few friendly words, Fellowship (left) deserts Everyman, who must go on his way alone.

Derived from a Dutch morality play written in the late 1400's, *Everyman* became the most famous of all English ecclesiastical dramas, and has been performed continuously by schools and churches all over the world. In his long journey toward the grave, Everyman seeks such companions as Fellowship, Worldly Goods, Strength, Beauty, The Fives Senses, Good Deeds, and Knowledge. But, symbolic of all Christian teaching, Good Deeds alone accompanies him to the Kingdom of Heaven.

Everyman kneels before his friend Knowledge, who never deserts him on earth. The sleeping figure represents Good Deeds who will arise to accompany Everyman into Paradise.

The Elizabethans

So towering is the figure of Shakespeare on the skyline of world drama that he completely overshadows a host of brilliant contemporaries whose plays are among the finest ever written.

For half a century (1590-1640) a dazzling procession of poetic masterpieces crossed the bare boards of the little wooden theatres in Shoreditch and on the Bankside—the muddy, crime-infested outskirts of London. Here in a rowdy carnival atmosphere of bear and bull baiting a peculiar assortment of pickpockets, gentlemen, lackeys, merchants, noble rakes, and their consorts applauded, booed, interrupted a considerable body of the world's great poetry: Marlowe's *Faustus* and *Edward the Second,* Jonson's *Volpone* and *Alchemist,* Dekker's *Shoemaker's Holiday,* Heywood's *Woman Killed with Kindness,* Beaumont and Fletcher's *Maid's Tragedy,* John Webster's *Duchess of Malfi* and *White Devil,* Middleton & Rowley's *Changeling,* Massinger's *New Way to Pay Old Debts,* Ford's *Broken Heart.*

Yet apparently few if any of the 17th-century Englishmen who saw or read these plays suspected that they were "not of an age, but for all time." Not even the playwrights themselves, who sold their plays outright to the theatre owners for a few paltry pounds, had any idea that their work was literature—none save Ben Jonson who was ridiculed by his fellows because he collected and published his own plays.

And though the dramatists have long since been accorded their proper place in the literary firmament, there are those who still cannot reconcile such divine poetry with such mercenary origins. Hardly a year passes without the publication of a new volume purporting to prove that some scholar-aristocrat wrote Shakespeare's plays. The authors cannot believe they were written by an actor—the son of a glove-maker—for a stock company.

We today can probably best understand Elizabethan drama by noting the astonishingly close parallel to a phenomenon of our century—the Hollywood film. Both had "low-brow" origins. The men who organized the King's Company and the Admiral's Men and who built the first English theatres did not come from "the upper classes," the universities, the literary milieu of Edmund Spenser and Francis Bacon. Neither were the men who built the first Hollywood studios and made the first crude films honored or even known in academic circles.

Both were commercial enterprises, aimed solely at providing popular entertainment that would draw crowds and make money. Whatever differentiation the theatre and studio owners made between a bloody melodrama and *Hamlet,* between a Mack Sennett comedy and *Shoulder Arms,* was merely the difference in gate receipts.

Both were regarded by the eggheads as mere entertainment—the plays on a level with the bloody spectacles at the Bear Garden, the movies on a level with the World Series. *Volpone, The Duchess of Malfi, Henry IV* created no more ripple within the 16th-century cloisters of Oxford and Cambridge than did *Greed, The Merry Widow, The Gold Rush* within American university halls.

And so it was that Elizabethan devotees of literature and the arts—even as their American counterparts—were slow to realize that they were witnessing one of History's oldest pranks: the birth of great art in most unlikely places and of most unpromising parentage.

Julius Caesar

The vitality of *Julius Caesar,* written in 1599, increases with the centuries, as more thinking men become concerned with means and ends. The play is based on incidents taken from the Greek historian Plutarch, but its greatness lies in its noble verse and in the conception of its central figure, Brutus, whose great-hearted desire to keep Rome from dictatorship blinds him to the meanness of the conspirators who involve him in the killing of Caesar.

Amherst College gave *Caesar* in Elizabethan costume on a replica of a Shakespearean stage in the Folger Library, Washington, D.C.

A theatre-in-the-round production of *Caesar* was given with stylized settings at the Edison Hotel, New York, 1950.

King Richard II

The Tragedye of Richard II is the story of the downfall of a gay and passionate but wilful and ineffectual king who was deposed by Henry Bolingbroke and then killed in 1400. One of the latest (1597) of Shakespeare's English history plays, it draws heavily upon *Holinshed's Chronicles.* In some respects it is the first of the poet's tragedies of character, for young Richard, like King Lear, mistakes the trappings of Kingship for true authority, and is more to blame than anyone else for his own destruction.

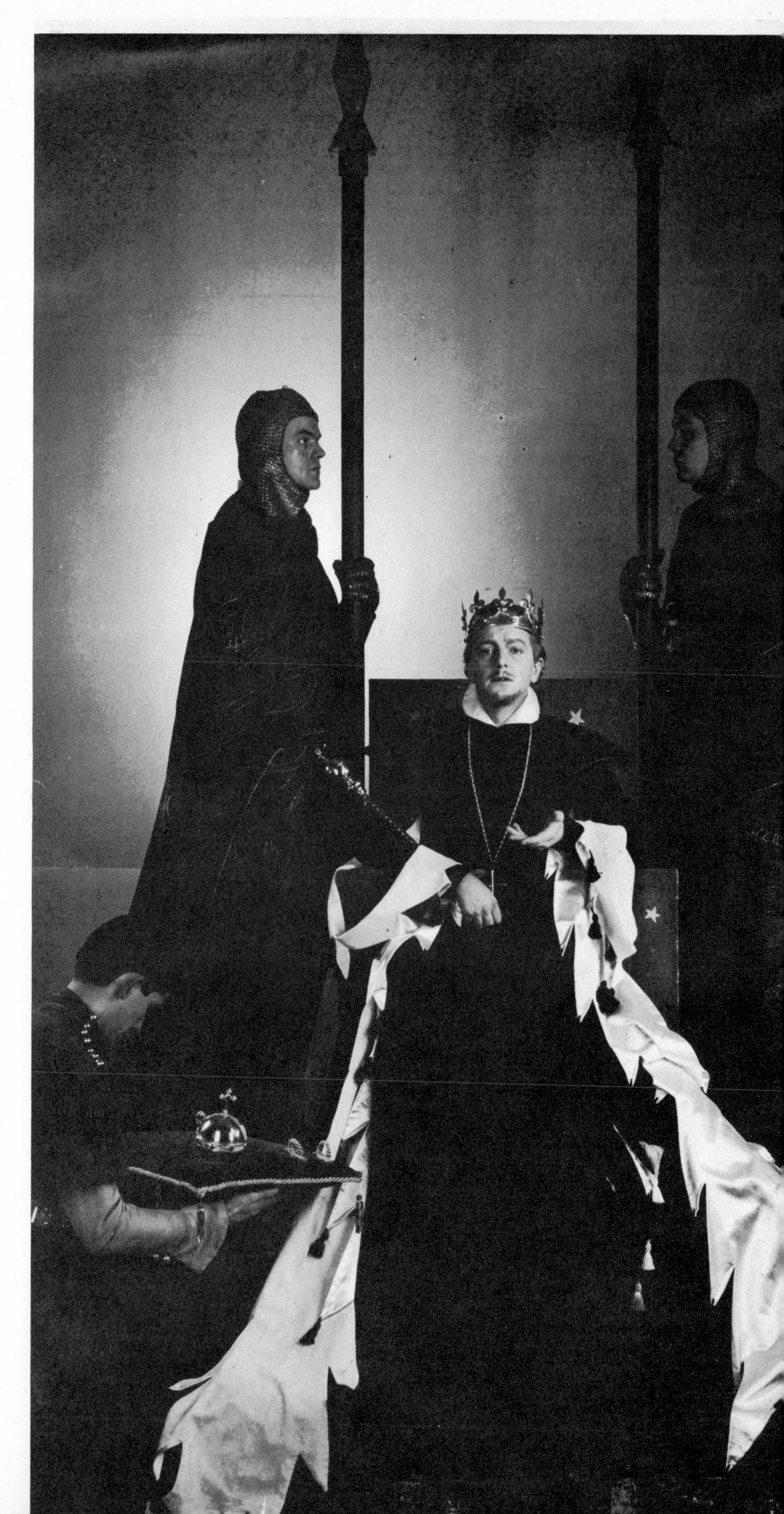

Maurice Evans excelled as this high-strung king when he himself produced the play on Broadway in 1937 and gave it its longest run—171 consecutive performances.

King Richard III

One of the bloodiest episodes in the Wars of the Roses—a century-long feud between two families for England's throne—occurred when Richard III killed off six people to grab the crown. Shakespeare's early play (1593), written around the deformed, malignant, and ghost-ridden figure of Richard himself, always hypnotizes an audience, and has attracted every notable actor from Richard Burbage, a friend of Shakespeare's, to John Barrymore.

The late John Barrymore made a wonderfully diabolic Richard in his 1920 production.

Parting is such sweet sorrow for these ecstatic lovers, who are locked in their last living embrace.

Romeo and Juliet

Romeo and Juliet, the most illustrious of star-crossed lovers, have been portrayed under many odd circumstances. In Shakespeare's day Juliet was acted by a boy. Later the title roles were played in London by the Cibbers, father and daughter, and by the Cushmans, sisters. In 1887 six actresses played Juliet in one performance, each appearing in one scene with a full-time Romeo. In the 1942 American production Sir Laurence Olivier and Vivian Leigh (above) made an ideally youthful and handsome couple, though they had not yet developed the acting skill which brought them later honors.

Henry IV

Perhaps the greatest achievement of London's Old Vic company, which Americans saw on Broadway in 1947, was its presentation of both parts of *Henry IV*. Written in 1597-98, they belong among Shakespeare's ten great historical dramas — a superlative tapestry of England's history from John to King Henry VIII.

The revolt against Henry IV was led by gallant young Hotspur, who is finally slain by his royal foe. But hulking above the battles stands a huge vat of a man named Falstaff. A complex mixture of weakness and strength, of honesty and lies, he is the first comic character to rise above mere buffoonery in the history of drama.

Hotspur (Sir Laurence Olivier) is as fiery a lover as he is a warrior. His adoring young wife was acted by Margaret Leighton.

Doll Tearsheet (Joyce Redman) is Shakespeare's most splendid tavern wench. Falstaff found her vastly to his liking.

Falstaff (Ralph Richardson) is the constant crony of the Prince of Wales (Michael Warre, right). But when the playboy Prince reforms, he coldly banishes the old tosspot from his presence.

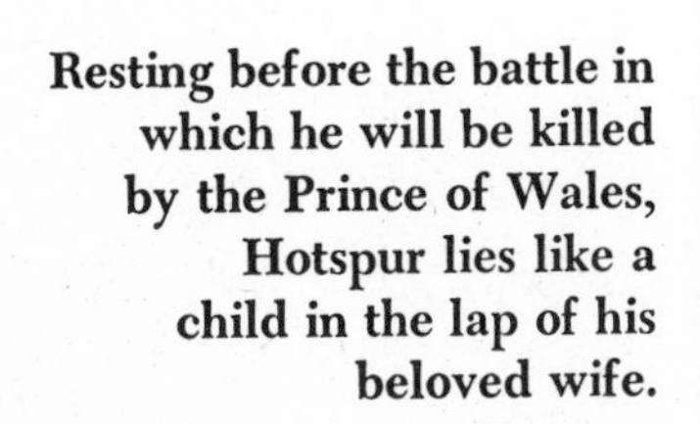

Resting before the battle in which he will be killed by the Prince of Wales, Hotspur lies like a child in the lap of his beloved wife.

"My heart is so sore," sings Henry VIII (Victor Jory), while courting Anne Bullen. Both words and music to this sad song were actually written by the King, England's most musical monarch.

Henry's new queen, Anne, is crowned in 1533 in Westminster Abbey. Three years later Henry had Anne beheaded after she had borne his child, Elizabeth, who became England's greatest queen.

Henry VIII

As a play *Henry VIII,* which was written jointly by Shakespeare and John Fletcher, is no masterpiece. But when it is properly produced, it can be a handsome pageant depicting a crucial time in Britain's history when Henry's unbridled passions brought him six wives and precipitated the break with Rome which marked the beginning of England's rise to power in Europe.

Henry VIII had its most satisfactory production on Broadway in 1948 by the new American Repertory Theater. This was the most distinguished effort to date to give the U.S. a regular program of fine plays, both on Broadway and on tour. Headed by Director Margaret Webster and such actors as Eva LeGallienne and Walter Hampton, it managed to produce plays by Shakespeare, Ibsen, Barrie, and Shaw before it disbanded after one unprofitable season.

The King holds court beside his first wife Katharine (Eva Le Gallienne). He is about to be hoodwinked by Cardinal Wolsey (Walter Hampton, seated) who sends a young henchman to poison Henry's mind about an innocent man who is the Cardinal's foe.

The play begins, as shown in this production acted by children, with a ship full of Neapolitans being wrecked on a magic isle.

The Tempest

Inhabitants of the isle include the deposed king, Prospero, who becomes a magician and acquires a high-flying sprite, Ariel, to fetch and carry for him.

The Tempest, written about 1611 after the agony of the great tragedies and the savage irony of the bitter comedies (*Timon of Athens, Troilus and Cressida*), was one of Shakespeare's last plays. Set in a magical sea-girt island, *The Tempest* has always been a designer's paradise, as suggested by these photographs of two productions, one given on Broadway in 1944 with settings by Motley, and another performed by children of the King Coit school. The Broadway version, directed by Margaret Webster, had ballerina Vera Zorina as Ariel and Canada Lee as the pathetic and beastly Caliban. But this production owed most to Arnold Moss. He brought sorcery and grandeur to Shakespeare's great poetry in the role of Prospero, the deposed king who turns scholar and magician, then forgives mankind for the treachery done him and discards his protective supernatural powers to live once more in the world of men.

In the children's version two ship-wrecked passengers, Trinculo and Stephano, drunkenly run afoul of the brutish Caliban who hatches with them a plot to kill Prospero.

In the Broadway version of the scene above, the plot-hatchers are spotted by Ariel, who, invisible to them, causes no end of confusion by pitching into the conversation.

Macbeth (Michael Redgrave) meets avenging Macduff and recalls the cry of the armed head on the heath, "Beware Macduff!"

Edith Evans, as that most notorious sleep-walker, moans, "All the perfumes of Arabia will not sweeten this little hand!"

Macbeth

The witches who open the tragedy do not send Macbeth to his doom. He was already en route—weak, treacherous, obsessed with ambition and married to a woman in whom there was little sun and much midnight.

Two productions of *Macbeth* are shown here: one with Maurice Evans and Judith Anderson (1942); another with Michael Redgrave and Edith Evans (1946).

The Maurice Evans and Judith Anderson witches cackle over the world's most revolting brew.

Macbeth (Evans), seeing Banquo's ghost, cries, "Prithee, see there!"

Hearing eerie shapes utter oblique prophecies, Macbeth (Redgrave) cries, "Let this pernicious hour stand aye accursed in the calendar!" It was—in his own calendar

Love's Labour's Lost

Only comic relief which the King permits during his studies is provided by a "fantastical Spaniard" named Armado and his pint-sized page, Moth.

This "immature" comedy of Shakespeare's youth (1588) had a smartly imaginative production by the Brattle Theater at Cambridge, Mass., and a year later by the New York Repertory Company. Directed by Albert Marre, it was mounted in Edwardian style, which somehow made it more plausible and more fun. A satire on Utopias, the play demonstrates the foolishness of stifling natural instincts. King Henry of Navarre and three cronies resolve to give up women and take up studies for three years. Four women wander in, and the fine intentions wander out.

The Princess of France —in black tie—visits the King. Shunned by him, she and her three ladies still enjoy hunting and a picnic.

A constable, a pedant, and a curate—all hangers-on of the King—enjoy a bachelor game of croquet and discuss the Princess and her hunting prowess.

Armado, despite his zeal to follow the King's celibate vows, is transfixed by one Jaquenetta's trim limb.

The Princess and her ladies affect disastrously the king and his continent companions. Dressed as Muscovites, they come to court the damsels.

The ladies are not won by this sudden change of heart, assigning to each wooer a year's labor by which to prove his love.

Forbes Robertson (1898)
was a patrician Hamlet.

Hamlet

John Barrymore (1922)
had an electrifying power and stature.

Leslie Howard (1936)
was fine-grained and appealing.

Jean Louis Barrault (1952)
was willfully neurotic.

Alec Guinness (1950)
was high-strung and biting.

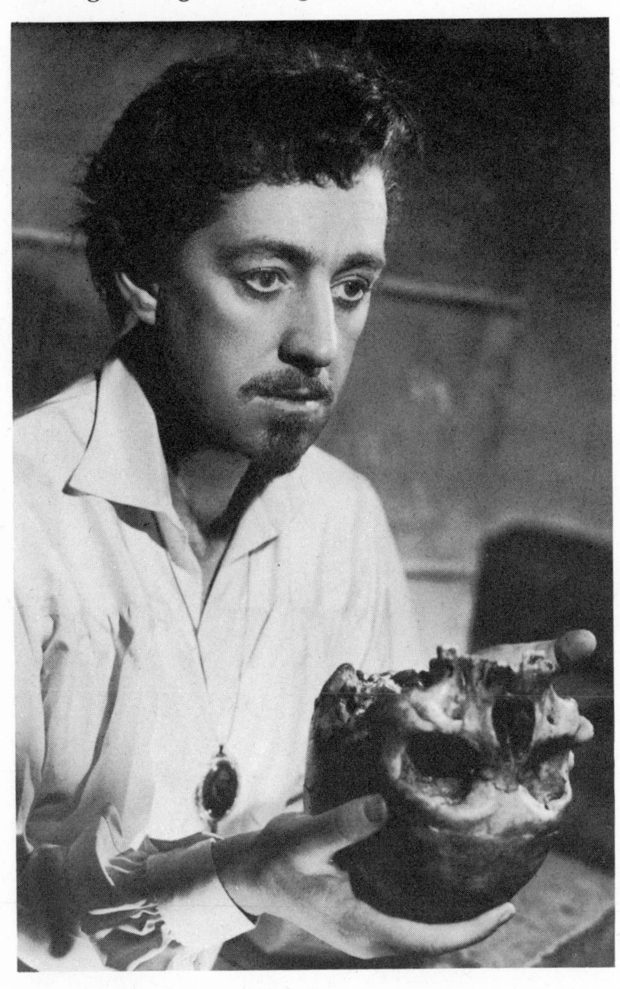

Ever since it was first produced in 1603, *Hamlet* has been an irresistible challenge to actors. Probably the greatest acting role ever conceived, it invites new styles of playing and new interpretations, and uses the full alphabet of acting skills. Part of its fascination comes from its intermingled strains of comedy and tragedy. For in no other serious play has Shakespeare so well integrated his comic relief. Humor and despair, light wit and dark reflection are bound together in Hamlet's character and point up its essential duality.

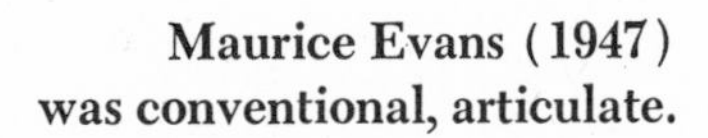

Maurice Evans (1947)
was conventional, articulate.

Othello

Insane with jealousy, Othello strangles his wife, and then, when he discovers that his suspicions were groundless, stabs himself, crying that he "loved not wisely but too well."

An Italian novella known to Shakespeare told of a Moorish captain who lets a sly officer trick him into doubting his wife's virtue; convinced of her guilt, he beats her to death "with a stocking filled with sand." Shakespeare turned this material into *Othello* (1604), the most powerful study of jealousy ever written. Its tragic hero, Othello, is driven to psychopathic jealousy of his chaste wife by flimsy evidence and whispered slanders. The arch slanderer, Iago, is a refreshing phenomenon to modern audiences who are accustomed to look for psychological motivations behind their villains. Iago is evil—simple, unmotivated, neat—the Devil himself. A 1942 production had José Ferrer as Iago, and Uta Hagen and Paul Robeson as the pitiful couple he destroys.

Iago goads Othello (left) to mistrust his wife by calling attention to her handkerchief being flaunted by the wench of her suspected lover. All this is cunningly concocted by Iago to rouse Othello's jealousy.

Katherine Hepburn acted Rosalind with great beauty in a Theater Guild production of this Shakespeare comedy. Dressed in masculine attire, she is supposed to hoodwink a number of people into believing she is a man—a likely story.

As You Like It

Rosalind in the forest of Arden dresses as a boy to escape a cruel father who wants her to marry against her will. Also to the forest—a kind of lovers' sanctuary—comes her true love, Orlando, escaping a cruel elder brother. Both Rosalind and the plot (lifted from a book by Thomas Lodge) make quite an ado over the fact that Orlando doesn't recognize her in boy's clothes. But after five acts of foolish mix-ups and superb verse, naught goes ill and every Jack has his Jill.

Plot and title for *Taming of the Shrew* were stolen from an anonymous play printed the same year that Shakespeare's comedy appeared (1594). But Shakespeare put into it the fireworks and fun that made his comedy the definitive lowdown on obdurate womanhood. Its hero, Petruchio, tames his caterwauling Kate by refusing to let her eat, lie down in, or wear anything but the best. Thus he managed to deprive her of food, clothing, sleep, and, finally, her shrewishness.

Taming of the Shrew

Alfred Lunt and Lynn Fontanne reviled and cuffed each other through the finest production the *Shrew* ever had: Theatre Guild, 1935.

Volpone

The dying Volpone (Morris Carnovsky opposite page) is suddenly resurrected when confronted by the seductive Celia who came to nurse him. Her scream, however, brings first aid from outside.

Volpone, a quirkish, complicated travesty on human greed written in 1610 by Ben Jonson, was the most successful 1951 production of Hollywood's skillful Actor's Laboratory. The play's villain, Volpone—the fox—extracts gifts from avaricious friends by pretending to be dying and promising to bequeath each of them his fortune. Helped by his sly servant Mosca (the mosquito), he gets one friend to compromise his young wife Celia (the dove), another to disinherit his son. In the end the trickster is out-tricked when Mosca gets his money and drives him out of town. Jonson's flawlessly constructed plays show more wit than Shakespeare's, but his characters lack depth. Like the wily Volpone and Celia, who is all cooing submissiveness, they are personifications of a single characteristic rather than real people.

Corvino accuses his wife, Celia, of having an affair with the old would-be invalid, Volpone. Corvino wants her to inherit Volpone's gold, but not go too far for it.

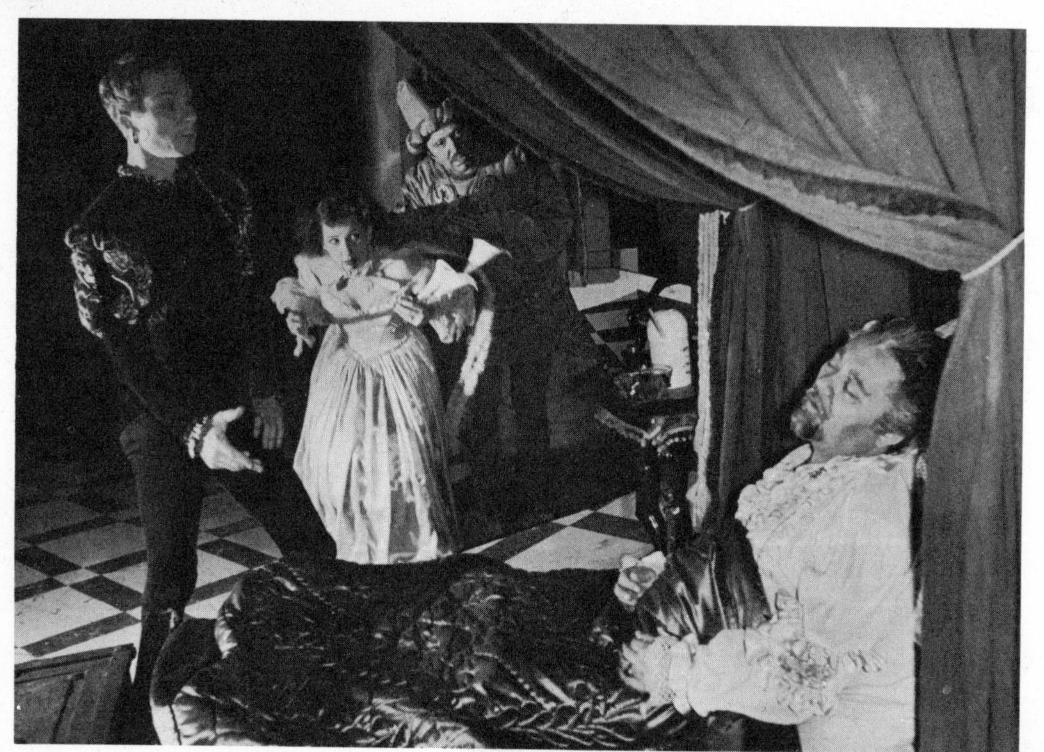

← Innocent Celia is led to Volpone's bedside by her greedy husband who bestows her upon the sick man. At left is the cynical servant, Mosca, who engineers the plot.

With Volpone "dead" (right), Mosca has the will read which makes him sole heir. But he agrees to share his wealth with the would-be inheritors, and Volpone, afraid of his foes, flees town.

The Duchess confronts her two wicked brothers, the Duke and Cardinal, while Antonio kisses her hand.

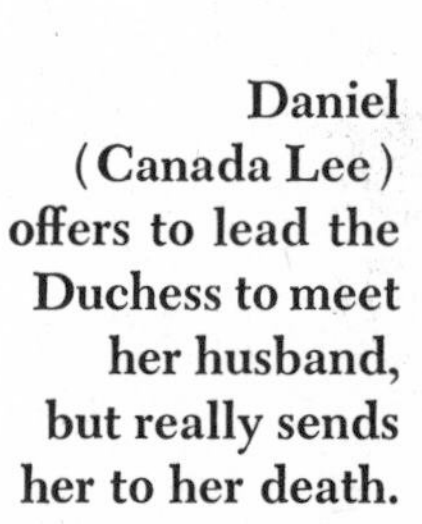

Daniel (Canada Lee) offers to lead the Duchess to meet her husband, but really sends her to her death.

At the end the Cardinal, ravi mad, is dying; his mistress lies dead; Daniel, fatally wounded, expires, and th Duke will soon be stabbed.

The Duchess of Malfi

The Duchess (Elisabeth Bergner) trusts Daniel, saying, "Your direction shall lead me by the hand."

John Webster's *Duchess of Malfi* (1613-14) tells of a lovely widowed duchess who, left with a fortune and three children on her hands, is remarried happily to one Antonio, a kindly steward in her castle. Her two evil brothers—a duke and a cardinal—set out to kill the young heirs, steal the fortune, and go on to compound the calamities until nine corpses strew the stage. Webster is called Shakespeare's great pupil in the art of tragedy and poetic power, but his *Duchess* has interest mainly as a shocker. In 1946 Elisabeth Bergner acted the Duchess, and the fine Negro actor, Canada Lee, played Daniel de Bosola, who pretended to befriend her, finally betrayed her.

Hooded assassins, employed by her brothers, are slowly strangling the little Duchess because she married against their wishes.

Theatre of the Orient

This short section on the Oriental Theatre contains examples from the Chinese and Japanese; nothing is available from such countries as Java, Siam, and India. Chinese theatre had the usual beginning in religious rites, with masked and chanting witch doctors, called Wu, propitiating the dieties that controlled weather and harvest, and giving wild war dances to celebrate victory. The brilliant Tang Emperor, Ming Huang (713-756), founded the first real theatre. He established a school of acting in his pear garden, and to this day actors are called "Young People of the Pear Garden," and burn incense before an image of Ming Huang that stands in every Chinese playhouse.

Instead of comedy and tragedy, Chinese plays have been classified as civil and military, and the majority of them are melodramas with a happy ending. Long and arduous training goes into the making of an actor, who must also be a singer, dancer, and acrobat. Until recently all actors were male, and many feminine roles are still played by men.

Stage settings are almost nonexistent, but there is an elaborate system of properties, including a language of flags. Four black flags mean a heavy storm; waves drawn on four flags indicate a body of water; if two flags decorated with wheels are carried, soneone is riding in a chariot; one flag carried by a single actor indicates a thousand soldiers. A general is always costumed magnificently with jewels, spangles, and embroidery. Four pennants are fastened to his shoulders and his headdress may carry feathers six feet long to indicate pride in victory.

Today three types of theatre exist in China. First, the Classical which still follows the ancient model and appeals to a majority of playgoers. Then there is the Western theatre that has flourished more than 30 years, presenting a repertory of occidental plays from Shakespeare to Shaw. Last, there is the new Yangko, or Theatre of the Revolution, which combines its own ideology with the Classical and Western.

While there is a tradition that Japanese drama originated in a ritual dance given to quell a volcanic eruption in 805, historical evidence indicates the theatre was brought into Japan from China. The Mother of Japanese Drama, Iso-no-Zenji, was famed for dancing in male attire.

The No plays, introduced in the fourteenth century, combined spoken lines, music, and dancing. They were about as long as a one-act play and were patronized mostly by the ruling caste. Still produced today, the No have a bewitched, marionette-like quality caused by rhythmic steps and gestures, fixed gaze of the masks, and unnatural voice tones. The effect is mesmerizing and sometimes frightening.

Popular entertainment for the people was provided by the Kabuki plays. They were introduced by O-Kuni, a stagestruck priestess who left a Shinto temple and went into the theatre where she reached the height of her immense popularity in 1603. She gathered about her a troupe of men and women who gave song and dance shows. Other Kabuki groups were formed, but the actors were regarded as such a disreputable lot that all Kabuki were shut down. Later a more settled group restored Kabuki and improved its quality in every way. Today the Kabuki theatre is vastly enjoyed by Western visitors, and is regarded as one of the most exciting types in post-war Japan. Both the stylized, traditional No plays and the flexible, lively Kabuki must take turns on the stage for the health of Japanese theatre.

Mary Martin as Tchao-ou-niang, a Chinese nun, cherishes the lute her husband left as a keepsake when he disappeared to seek fame as a scholar.

Lute Song

Acted for 500 years by strolling players and showboat troupes, this Chinese classic Pi-Pa-Ki (*Lute Song*), written by a 14th century schoolmaster, has perhaps had the longest continuous run of any play in stage history. It concerns a perfect wife whose husband leaves her to become a scholar and, against his will, is forced to marry a proud princess. Staying at home to nurse his aged parents, the wife becomes a beggar and a nun before the gods reunite her with her husband. Produced on Broadway in 1946 with versatile Mary Martin as the wife, *Lute Song* lost some of its folk-tale simplicity, but the timeless appeal of its story and the lovely costumes and sets by Robert Edmond Jones made it a fascinating stage experiment.

Tchao-ou-niang bids farewell to her beloved husband (Yul Brynner).

Guards of the palace, where the husband now resides as a court scholar, keep him from returning to his wife.

The gods take mercy on the pious wife, help her provide a tomb for her deceased in-laws, and chart her happiness.

The princess (Helen Craig), who wed the scholar, finally meets his first wife, and nobly helps the couple to reunite.

The wicked sea serpent, created by an actress sticking her head through a curtain, wails as the gods curtail her powers and sentence her to stay forever beneath the sea.

Chinese Theatre

The venerable Chinese theatre was represented in 1950 by the Sun Sing playhouse in New York's Chinatown. It offered a repertory of some 360 Chinese plays, usually based on folklore, and sprinkled with songs and dances which the actors, amazingly, knew by heart. Plays were performed against modernized backdrops, but still used the elaborate symbolism established in China 1400 years ago. An orchestra officiated on stage; property men strolled unconcerned among the actors. Lamentably, the Sun Sing recently closed.

The Dragon's Revenge concerns some gods who meet to consider the crimes of a sea serpent (opposite page). The serpent is guilty of ousting a good dragon from his den, and he takes female form to seduce young men. Some actors play male and female parts interchangeably: the white-bearded god is a woman.

In a short play called *The Beautiful Butterflies* a righteous Tiger God does a sword dance to frighten several young ladies who represent evil butterflies.

Angry monks roll on the floor in sympathy with their priest after he has lost control over the drought and the rain pours down.

A lady is sent to win over a high priest (standing) who is causing a drought. Caught by his monks, she threatens suicide, but they restrain her.

Kabuki

Tokyo's Kabuki theatre includes in its vast repertory of plays, skits, and dance acts, this little drama called *A Wrathful God*, based on a folk tale. It begins when a touchy high priest of the Court, offended because his ambitions were thwarted, flees to the mountains where he confines the rain dragons, causing a universal drought. The Court sends a fair lady to seduce him and break his spell over the rain. Plying him with wine (symbolic of marriage), she gets him so befuddled that he falls asleep. Then she releases the rain dragons and escapes in the downpour. She is portrayed by a male actor, Kumitaro, one of Japan's great interpreters of feminine roles.

Renewing her efforts to seduce the high priest, she lures him into a wine-drinking rite, and he loses his powers over the rain.

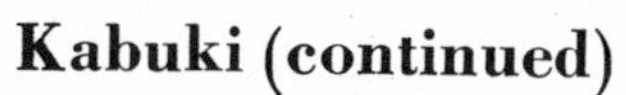

Kabuki (continued)

In his moment of supreme fury the high priest, surrounded by his monks, realizes that he has been duped by a beautiful siren, and the rain dragons are on the loose.

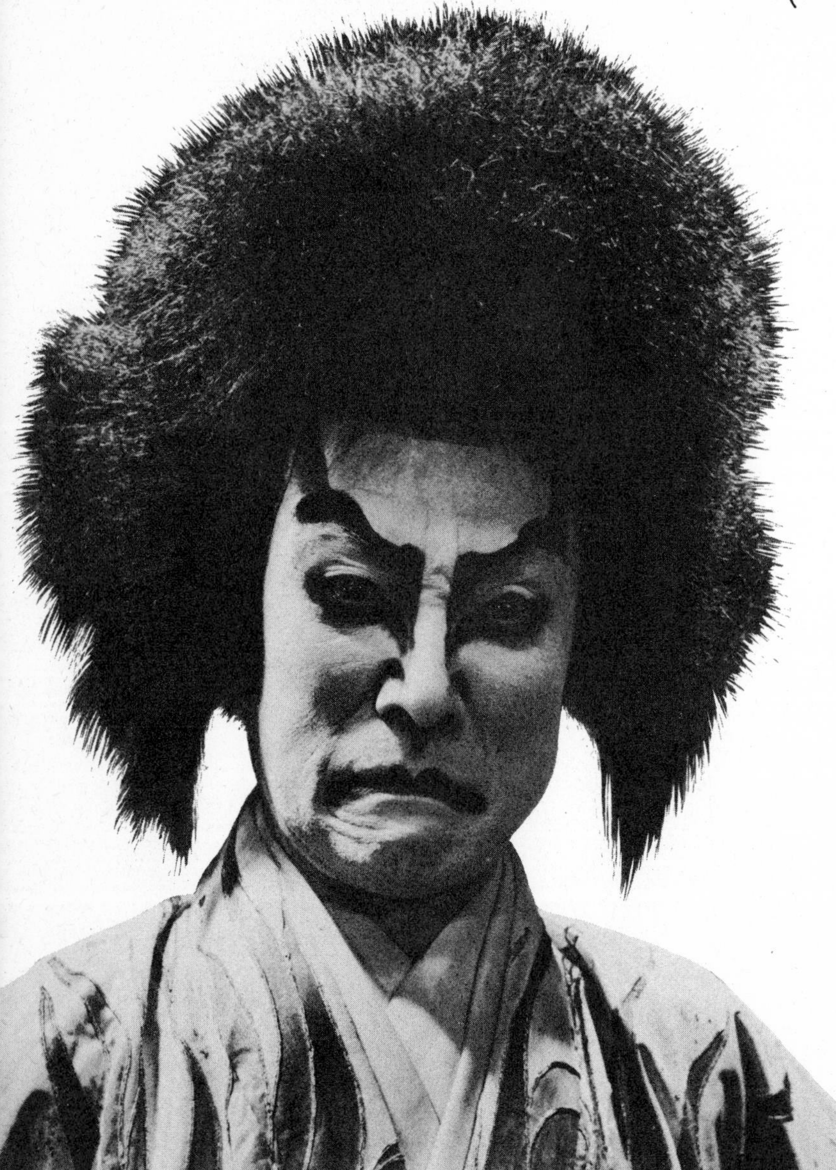

The high priest is played by Chojuro Kawarsaki, who masters the great art of Japanese stage make-up. For his final wrath (his peaceful mien is shown on the preceding page), he wears a frightening wig, and adds baleful black lines to eyes, nose, and mouth.

Poetry and Protest Abroad

Beginning with the seventeenth century, France held the stage first with the poetic dramatists, Corneille and Racine, both of whom used the classical plays, especially Greek, as their models.

It took Molière to write poetic plays that are full of protest. He did not attack tyrants nor public outrages, but with wit and genius pounced upon human failings: hypocrisy, intellectual snobbery, hypochondria, *nouveaux riches.* His plays are enjoyed today because these failings are still ubiquitous.

Le Sage wrote *Turcaret* (1709) which condemned the grasping rich; and in 1748 Beaumarchais wrote *The Barber of Seville* as a protest against overbearing police measures. The Revolution was near, to be followed by a bleak period in the French theatre.

Victor Hugo strode into the eighteen thirties as a champion of Romanticism and an enemy of the psuedo-classical. *Hernani,* despite its being good poetry, caused a historic brawl. *Le Roi S'amuse* was banned for being anti-royalist and pro-republican.

Out of Germany came the great Johann Wolfgang von Goethe with *Faust,* one of the most profound poetic dramas of all time, not so much a protest as a gospel full of occult wisdom.

Henrik Ibsen of Norway was a towering figure in the drama. Only two of his plays, *Brand* and *Peer Gynt,* are in verse; the rest are prose works which bristle with protest against lies, corruption, hypocrisy, and egomania. Ibsen can set a play in a modest home in a village and suggest that all is not well with the world.

The Russian physician, Anton Chekhov, was a quiet but powerful man of protest. He does not portray petty, spineless types, but people who would get along all right with a little luck in a less barren setting. He saw not only the benumbing social order of Old Russia, but the down-drag, hopeless monotony that comes with too much civilization.

Italian Luigi Pirandello has somewhat the same idea of the bewildered fumbling of people who don't know what they are looking at, or what to do about it. His *Six Characters in Search of an Author* and *As you Desire Me* are among the finest modern plays.

The Spanish writer of melodrama, José Echegaray, won the Nobel Prize for Literature in 1904. Jacinto Benavente, the greatest name in contemporary Spanish theatre, is a man of great erudition, who can use romanticism or realism, kindness or cynicism, with equal brilliance.

Karel Capek of Czechoslovakia created in *R.U.R.* a spirited piece of protest against the Machine Man, or perhaps Nazism; and with his brother, Josef, wrote *The Insect Comedy* pointing out the littleness of mankind.

While there have been many good plays written in Europe in the last quarter-century, there has been so much real drama, much of it "Blood Tragedy," that protest has taken the form of hurling invective or bombs. Poetry does not flourish under an iron heel.

The Would-Be Gentleman

One of Moliere's brilliantly comic criticisms of the social artifices of his day, *The Would-Be Gentleman* (1670) lost its sting when it was modernized for Bobby Clark. But as the *nouveau riche* Monsieur Jordain, who yearned to acquire culture and social grace, Bobby had himself a hilarious romp.

Bobby learns elegant dancing from two hired teachers (Harrison and Fisher).

He is literally carried away by the beauty of the ballet.

He almost swoons from the sheer wizardry of his own grace.

He loves dancing, but he would love more to lead away the pretty dancer.

He manipulates his lips to produce some élite diction.

A real gentleman must be a model of sartorial refinement.
Bobby is sure he is.

In a sulphurous orgy of ghouls and sirens, Faust is seduced by a wench in flowing draperies, while his pure-hearted sweetheart, Margarete, watches him from the high ground by the trunk of a sinister tree.

Signing the Devil's pact with his own blood, Faust, the ambitious scholar, pricks his wrist and sucks the wound while the Devil watches triumphantly.

The Devil leads Faust into a nightmare world of ghastly demons and tormented spirits.

Faust is dragged away to Hell by the Devil after he has corrupted his sweetheart, Margarete. But there is hope that her love may redeem him.

Goethe's Faust

For most of his life Germany's great thinker, Johann Wolfgang von Goethe worked on his two-part poetic drama, *Faust*. Based on ancient legend, *Faust* is a Christian allegory of man's quest for truth and his preoccupation with worldly things at the expense of his soul. Seldom produced, *Faust* was handsomely presented at Yale University's School of the Drama in 1949, the 200th anniversary of Goethe's birth.

In a 1930 production Alla Nazimova played Mrs. Alving, who must watch her son go mad because of his father's vices.

Ghosts

Norway's great Henrik Ibsen, attacking the sins of society with savage vigor, had incalculable influence on modern play-writing. His famous *Ghosts* was an indictment of dishonest society which sanctioned a man concealing the fact he had contracted syphilis. Transmitted by heredity to his innocent son, the disease brought despair and insanity.

The Father

With this outcry against domineering women, Sweden's August Strindberg in 1887 won international fame. His heroine, plotting to get control of her child, insinuates to her husband that he is not its father, that he is a weakling, that he will soon go insane. He ends up in a straitjacket and dies in a fit of impotent fury.

In a 1948 Broadway production Mady Christians played the female viper and Raymond Massey was her victim.

The Cherry Orchard

Anton Chekhov's masterpiece, *The Cherry Orchard* (1903), supposedly presages the decline of Russian aristocracy just before the revolution. Indeed

The prosperous peasant, Lopahin, tells Leonid and his charming sister, Lyubov, who has just returned from a gay Moscow visit, that their estate can be saved if they will cut up the orchard into lots.

"Oh, my orchard!" sighs Lyubov, gazing at the frail blossoms. "After the dark, stormy autumn and the cold winter, you are young again." Leonid sadly reminds her the orchard will be sold to pay their debts.

its high-bred heroine, Lyubov, who is unable to face the reality of selling her cherry orchard to save her ancestral estate correctly symbolizes the aristocratic dilemma. But Chekhov's play rises above its implicit judgments, and its characters speak not as symbols but as living people who, for all their frailties, are more beautiful and more important than what happens to them. The play's fourth Broadway revival was in 1943. Directed by Margaret Webster, it starred Eva LeGallienne and Joseph Schildkraut as Lyubov and Leonid.

Sad irony permeates this scene at dusk (top) where a bookkeeper mournfully strums a guitar to woo his love, who prefers a faithless valet, while a bored governess watches all three.

A dance (right) is given by Lyubov while her brother and Lopahin go to the auction of the estate. Although she cannot pay the musicians, she still refuses to admit the estate must go.

"My beautiful orchard . . . goodbye," cries Lyubov, as she and her brother are about to leave their home.

The faithful valet, Firs, lies forgotten in the house scarcely hearing the axes in the orchard and the workers singing.

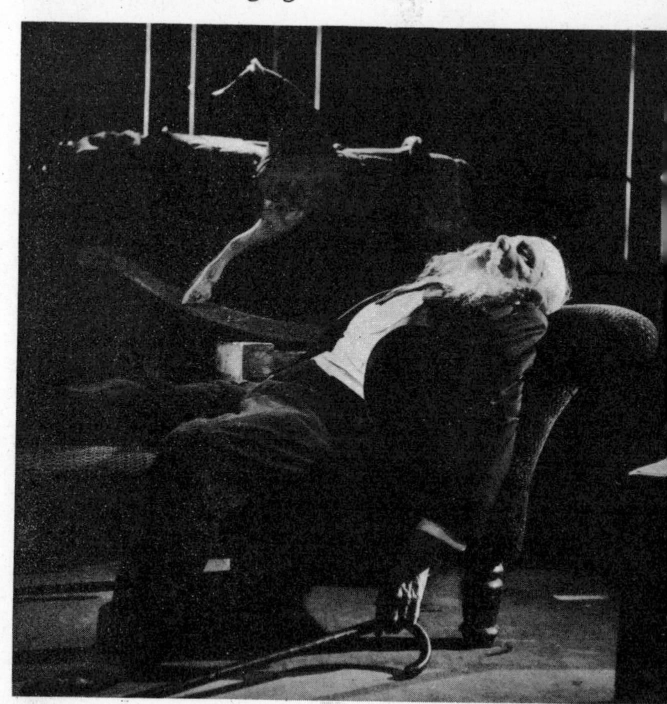

In this great drama of frustration the three sisters are (left to right): Olga (Judith Anderson), Masha (Katharine Cornell), and Irina (Gertrude Musgrove).

The Three Sisters

One of the most impressive theatre events in Broadway history was a 1942 revival of Chekhov's drama, directed by Guthrie McClintic. With even more variety and richness than usual, Chekhov created a sort of three-part fugue of interweaving themes and feelings. It conveyed the story of three sisters from a once wealthy family whose discontent with their static provincial life is expressed by an unfulfilled longing to return to the gay Moscow of their youth. The cast included Katharine Cornell, Judith Anderson, Ruth Gordon, Gertrude Musgrove, Dennis King, Edmund Gwenn, and Tom Powers.

On Irina's 30th birthday, goateed Dr. Chebutykin (Edmund Gwenn) presents her with a silver samovar. The doctor, given to drinking and reading the papers, lives with the three orphaned sisters in their big provincial house.

Professing love for Irina, Baron Tuzenbach (Alexander Knox), attached to the local army post, is interrupted by Natasha (Ruth Gordon), a vulgar town girl who is being fervently courted by Andrey, the sisters' brother.

At the birthday lunch a toast is proposed by Masha's schoolteacher husband (Tom Powers). Around the table are family members, the old nurse, Natasha, Dr. Chebutykin, and friends from the army post.

The Three Sisters (continued)

Scheming to control the house, Natasha, who has now married Andrey (Eric Dressler), asks if his sister Irina can be made to give up her large warm room to their baby son.

In the garden the doctor and Irina twit Masha's husband about shaving his mustache. Andrey, whose wife has killed his dreams of being a great scientist, wheels his child around the grounds.

Drunk and moaning miserably, the doctor staggers into the girls' upstairs sitting room. The knowledge that a patient has died because of his inadequacies makes him realize he is a failure.

Saying goodbye are Masha and her lover (Dennis King). With Irina's baron killed and Olga (right) made school headmistress, the sisters are doomed to a life of boredom.

Crime and Punishment

The streets of Petersburg, sprawling with drunkards and lost women, made the world Raskolnikov wished to escape from.

The passionate turmoil of Fyodor Dostoevsky's novels has attracted many attempts to compress them on to the stage. One such was Rodney Ackland's version of *Crime and Punishment,* which was produced in 1947, with John Gielgud and Lillian Gish in leading roles. On a cluttered stage full of shadows and noise, the student Raskolnikov lives out his tragic progression from arrogance to murder, remorse, final salvation.

The murderer on his couch listens to gossip about his crime by friends whose faces are distorted in this photograph to mirror his image of them.

Leah is taken to a counsel of Rabbis who try to cast out the dybbuk. But Leah and her lover cannot be parted.

The Dybbuk

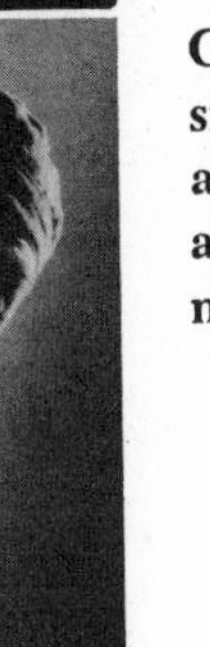

Custom permits these sinister beggars to attend the wedding feast and dance with the miserable bride, Leah.

Faint with fatigue, Leah (below) cries, "They kept turning and turning around me, and clutched me to them with their cold, withered hands."

One of the greatest Jewish plays, *The Dybbuk,* written in 1926 by S. Ansky, was given on Broadway in 1952 by the distinguished Habimah repertory theatre of Palestine. *The Dybbuk* (soul of one dead) is the wonderfully fantastic love story of Leah and Channon, who are kept from marrying when Leah's greedy father orders her to wed a wizened, rich youth. The soul of Channon, who dies of sorrow, enters Leah's body, causing her to speak with a man's voice and behave like one bewitched. The wisest rabbis in Russia try to drive out the spirit, but Leah herself abandons the earth and the lovers' souls are united.

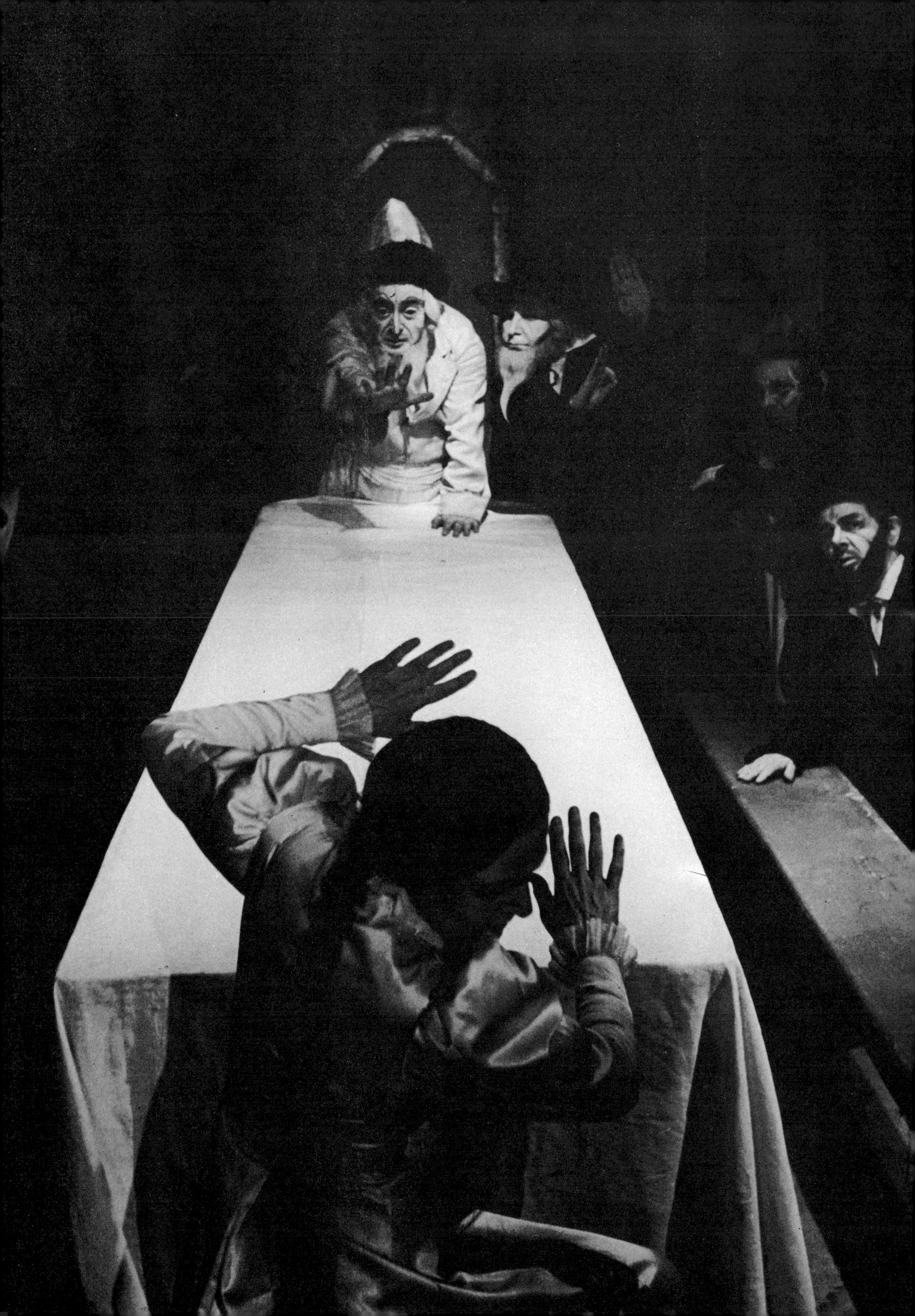

The

Sent to church
underwear, Schwe
weeps at t
Chaplain's serm
because "a repente
sinner was needed
Later he becomes t
Chaplain's orderl

Schweik (Michael Goldstein) is an unbelievably good-natured and honest rookie. More than that, he is also a symbol of tortured mankind, surrounded by the pomposity of generals, the corruption of empire, the inanity of doctors, the frailty of priests, the brutality of police.

Schweik, the dog vender, is arrested for treason because he predicts war will follow Archduke Ferdinand's assasination at Sarajevo. These medical experts send him to an insane asylum.

The general's widow, hearing of Schweik's attempt to enlist, regales him with roast chicken, which Schweik, starved on tea and aspirin, devours greedily.

Good Soldier Schweik

Schweik, the greatest fiction character to emerge from World War I, personifies the humble soldier whirled up out of war's insanity. He was born in a novel by the Czech journalist, Jaroslav Hasek. Czech soldiers, reading the first chapters in 1916, burst out laughing and refused to fight. Later the great German director Piscator made a popular, episodic play out of Schweik, given in New York in 1937 by the small Yiddish Artef Theater.

chweik reaches the front find many friends dead. He puts on gas mask because he is convinced he war stinks, and is soon mistakenly captured by his own troops.

Roxanne thinks Christian is the serenader, while Cyrano, hidden, sings the lays he wrote himself.

A late product of French romanticism, Edmond Rostand's great showpiece (1897) irresistably blends hokum and heroics. Big-nosed Cyrano is too ugly to win fair Roxanne. Seeing her fall in love with handsome Christian, Cyrano pens her songs and love letters which he nobly gives to his rival so he can win her himself. José Ferrer starred in a 1950 Broadway revival.

Cyrano de

Christian dies in battle just as he begins to suspect Roxanne really loves Cyrano. But Cyrano still feels he is unworthy of her love.

Bergerac

Roxanne comforts Cyrano who, wounded, is tended by nuns. Cyrano to Death: "... shod with marble ... gloved with lead ... let the old fellow come ... he shall find me sword in hand."

A fanatic young Communist (seated) and his wife submit to a search of their room by a party boss, whom the young man has been ordered to kill.

Red Gloves

Another Sartre melodrama, *Les Mains Sales,* translated into English as *Red Gloves,* played ambiguously with the great political problems of the time. It was a drama of conscience (should tyrants be murdered?) combined with one of sex (should tyrants be allowed to sleep with one's wife?). Neither question is satisfactorily answered, for the young man who is tormented by both does kill the tyrant, only to learn later that his jealousy was misplaced and his political ideas cockeyed.

He shoots the boss, not for political reasons, but because he suspects the boss is his wife's lover.

After two years in jail, the Communist is sent to death by his former friends because party-line changes have made a hero out of the dead tyrant.

Charles Boyer plays the Communist boss who is assassinated by his own party members because they think he is too liberal, but posthumously is made a hero.

The Respectful Prostitute

Lynchers appear as evil shadows across the wall of the bungalow where the prostitute is shielding the Negro.

French drama at the end of World War II was overcast by a murky mixture of philosophy and melodrama known as Existentialism. Jean-Paul Sartre was the master of the movement, and his biggest popular success was *The Respectful Prostitute,* which was produced on Broadway in 1948. The prostitute of the title, a small-town Southern floozy, turns heroic as she tries to save a fugitive Negro from lynching; but the cynicism and brutality of the respectable whites drag her back to her old profession.

A senator's son, a criminal in his own right, pulls a gun on the Negro.

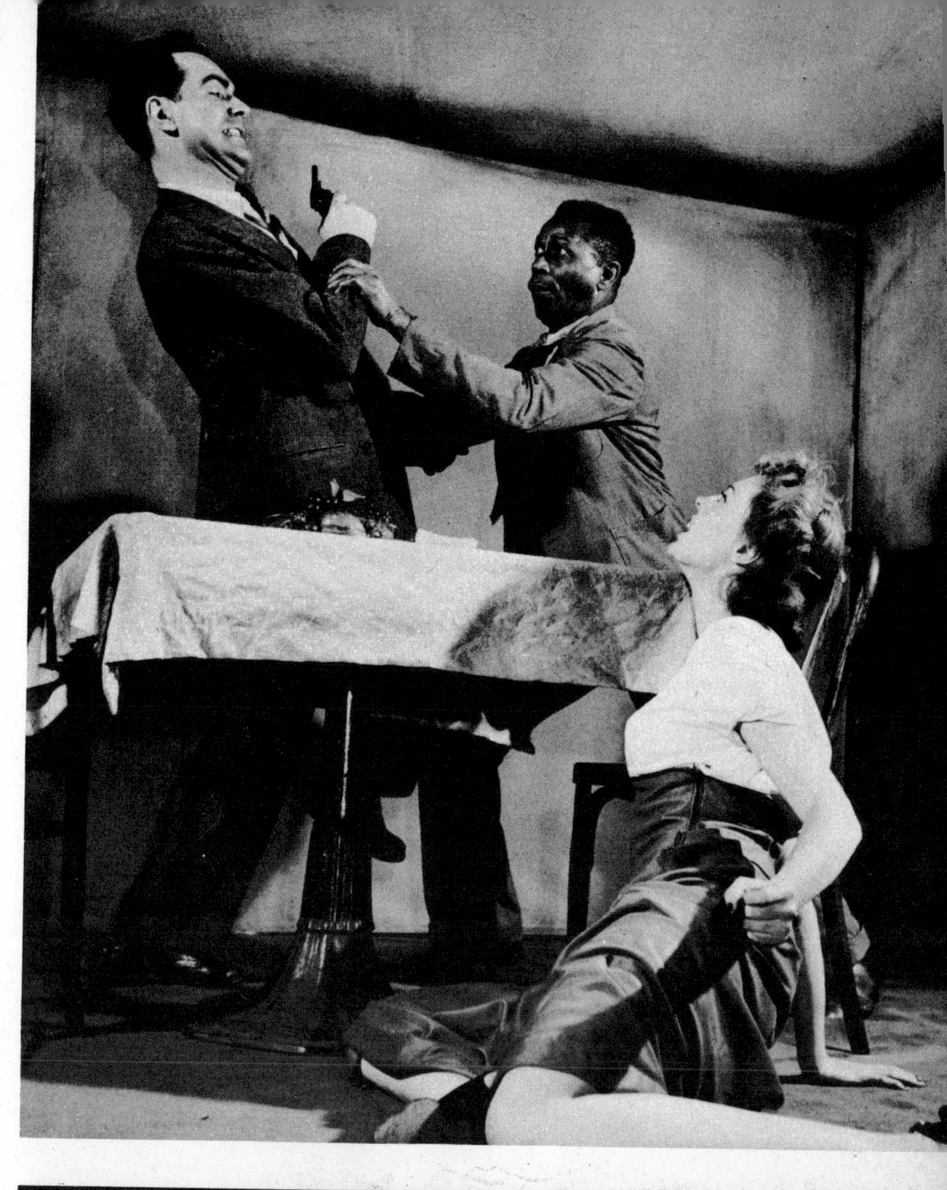

Meg Mundy played the role of the prostitute on Broadway.

"You're a murderer," screams the prostitute after the lynching. But she ends up in the murderer's arms.

The accused, Joseph K——, played by Jean Louis Barrault, stands before the head jailor, who tells him he must find out for himself what his crime is.

The Trial

In the endless halls of justice, Joseph K—— sees others like himself waiting to be tried for unknown crimes. Some have waited patiently for years.

Joseph seeks solace with a companion (Marie-Helene Daste), but is haunted by his accusers and by his feelings of nameless guilt.

From Franz Kafka's renowned novel *The Trial,* André Gide and Jean Louis Barrault created a play which was a Paris sensation in 1947 and came to Broadway with the Barrault repertory in 1952. *The Trial* presents the nightmarish effect upon one individual, Joseph K——, of the complexities of modern life. Joseph is an insignificant little bank clerk who wakes up one morning to find himself arrested for a crime of which neither he nor his judges have any knowledge.

In the end Joseph is put to death by weird executioners, but his crime is still a secret, not only to himself but to the rest of the world.

As the madwoman orates at her café, its denizens listen affectionately—all but a group of businessmen.

Four plutocrats work out their schemes, but the madwoman, behind, eavesdrops and decides to foil them.

At the madwoman's tea party, one friend chats with an imaginary dog, another addresses a nonexistent crowd.

Jean Giraudoux, the most impressive playwright of modern France, made the cafés and cellars of Paris the setting for a philosophic fantasy. His madwoman (played in New York in 1949 by Martita Hunt) is a frumpy old Parisienne who reigns over a café in the Chaillot district. When she overhears some plutocrats conspiring to dig for oil underneath Paris, she moves against them, neatly disposes of plots and plutocrats, along with a cluster of money-grabbing beauties. Underneath the lunacy of his dialogue and the complications of his story, Giraudoux deftly but distinctly gives answers to how evil is to be met and greed to be properly paid off.

Madwoman consigns money and beauties—"world's most powerful pressure group"—to a bottomless pit.

The Madwoman of Chaillot

The trio, shipwrecked in evening clothes, make the best of island life. The wife (Joan Tetzel) explains things to her husband (Robert Morley) while her lover acts as lookout.

The Little Hut

The wife, a snobbish type, keeps herself immaculately groomed in primitive surroundings.

A savage threatens to kill the men unless the wife yields to him. With a show of self-sacrifice, she agrees but the two men complain that she seems pleased at this way of saving their lives.

In *The Little Hut,* André Roussin, one of the more successful playwrights of the French theatre, made a desert island a setting for a scandalous and hilarious uninhibited spoof on 20th century marriages. Marooned on the island with a dull husband and a dashing lover, an attractive woman allots herself equally to the men, arranging to spend one week in their thatched hut as mistress, one week as wife. This open acknowledgment of illicit love disturbs the lover more than the husband—then a savage comes in to disturb them both.

Carried to the hut, the wife beams on the savage but rebuffs him when he turns out to be a ship's cook in disguise.

Saved, they say goodbye to the isle and a friendly ape, glad to get back to civilized hypocrisy.

Dying and almost blind, Galileo (left) gives his great treatise to be smuggled out of Rome and into the ages.

Galileo

Pope Urban VIII calls Galileo, "The light of Italy." The Inquisitor is bitterly intolerant. (The Papal vestments are kept on form in center.)

Galileo, called in to exhibit his telescope to young Prince Cosimo di Medici, is sent away without being allowed to show it.

Bertholt Brecht is Germany's leading contemporary dramatist. After Charles Laughton translated *Galileo,* in 1947, he played the star role in Hollywood, and later on Broadway. Here is the story of the great scientist who held "the earth rolls round the sun . . . and mothers, captains, scholars, Princes and Pope, are rolling with it." Good for him to provide Padua with a first-rate water pump; but ideas like that—heresy! Only by retracting was Galileo allowed to live—in confinement. The man who carried the *Discorsi* to Holland said, "This will be the cornerstone of a new physics."

All Fools Day revellers carry a huge effigy of Galileo, and shout, "The Bible Killer!"

To get money for Julie, who is having a child, Liliom conspires with a crony to rob a rich man. The hold-up fails and Liliom is shot by the police.

Julie is warned by police that Liliom (Burgess Meredith), who has just picked her up on a Budapest park bench, is a no-good bum. But she adores him anyway.

Dying from bullet wounds, Liliom reaffirms his love for Julie, who is soon to give birth to their daughter.

Liliom

In a poetic interlude, Liliom gets a permit from the Magistrate in heaven to return briefly to earth and give his child a star as a token of his love.

First produced in Budapest in 1908, *Liliom* was one of the few flops by Hungary's brilliant Ferenc Molnar. It became a great European hit after World War I, and Broadway loved it in 1921 under the aegis of The Theater Guild. Its 1947 revival had Ingrid Bergman as the angelic peasant girl who falls for Liliom, a Hungarian word meaning "roughneck." A charming mixture of fantasy and realism, *Liliom* was happily destined to become the Rodgers and Hammerstein 1944 musical, *Carrousel.*

The Play's The Thing

In this minor classic, revived on Broadway in 1948, Molnar's plot ripples around a kindly dramatist. He hastily writes a play so an actress friend can, by performing in it, convince a jealous suitor that the compromising dialogue he overheard was actually a rehearsal for the play.

The glamorous actress Ilona (Faye Emerson) acts out a romantic scene with her former lover (Arthur Margetson), written by the dramatist, Sandor (Louis Calhern). By this stratagem, Ilona clears her reputation so she can wed Sandor's godson, whom she really loves.

The English Comic Genius

English theatre since Ben Jonson has been largely a theatre of comedy. Good comedy usually involves criticism and freedom; self-criticism and controlled freedom are part of the English genius. The Magna Charta, House of Commons, Anglican church, and corner pub might all have been designed to liberate the human spirit for laughter.

When the monarchy was restored in 1660, the stage had lain in a coma for eleven years. When Charles II took the throne, there were only two theatres left in London, and people had lost the habit of playgoing. Restoration audiences were made up of the fashionable set—satellites, rakes, ladies of the evening, and the newly rich. They were ready for plays full of wit, intrigue, and sex; and to add to this high fare, for the first time women actors were employed instead of boys, who through the ages had played feminine roles.

In 1664 Etherege led off with *Love in a Tub,* the first of the Restoration comedies—comedies in which repartee and worldly women would glitter on the stage for half a century. When "Brawny" Wycherley tossed off *The Country Wife* and *The Plain Dealer,* adultery was just about the whole show. The comedy of manners reached its zenith with Congreve. In the well-concocted plots of such plays as *The Way of the World* and *Love for Love* his characters move about the stage like galvanized Dresden china figures, wired for dazzling light and sound effects. The Restoration's last dramatist, George Farquhar, whose death at 29 was a loss to the world, was moving out of the drawing room into the country-side. *The Beaux' Stratagem* is his last and best play.

Once again the bawdiness of the drama provoked such howls that Comedy, like an unmanageable jade, was shooed off the stage for about 60 years, until Oliver Goldsmith led her back with *She Stoops to Conquer.* Then came Richard B. Sheridan, who in *The Rivals* and *The School for Scandal* only hinted at wicked escapades and enlivened his comedies with eccentric characters and farcical mix-ups.

For a century comedy was lusterless until Gilbert and Sullivan showed up, representing the ancient school of Aristophanes. To be sure, they lacked the old rogue's epic lewdness, but they did not lack his gift for irreverence. They gave England a wonderful look at her own stupidities, to music.

Born in the same year, 1856, were two Irishmen: Oscar Wilde and Bernard Shaw. Wilde, destined to be outlived 50 years by his contemporary, was the larger man and the lesser figure. His famous epigrams are never really wise; but they have innuendos of wisdom. His *Importance of Being Earnest* is almost a perfect work of art.

George Bernard Shaw is a volcano, pouring out all sorts of matter; some of it slag and ashes, much of it rocks aimed at blockheads down in the valley, and some of it gold and gems. He was the most resourceful reformer of our time, and spoke in the most persuasive way—parable-telling. Another Irishman, John Synge, has been called the greatest of his nation's dramatists. The best of his plays, *Playboy of the Western World,* is full of poetry, malice, brashness, and magic.

In Somerset Maugham and Noel Coward England has produced two more writers who in Coward's words have "a talent to amuse." Maugham has more solidity, Coward more sparkle. But the most distinguished of the whole modern brotherhood are the American-born T. S. Eliot (he calls *The Cocktail Party* a comedy) and Christopher Fry. They unite laughter and wisdom—a marriage made in heaven.

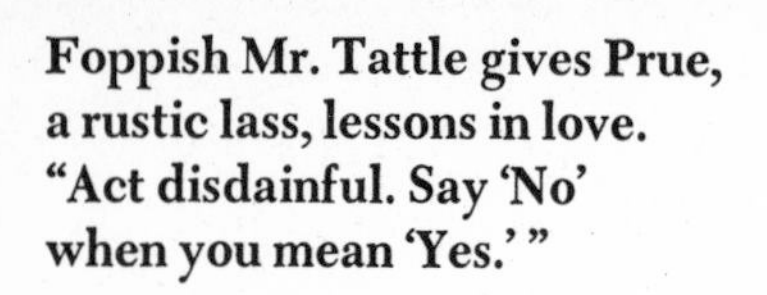

Foppish Mr. Tattle gives Prue, a rustic lass, lessons in love. "Act disdainful. Say 'No' when you mean 'Yes.' "

Disdain is forgotten. Prue tells her up-ended tutor, "I like it better than our old-fashioned country way."

"Make me happy by giving me a kiss," says Tattle. Prue says, "No." Then, following her lessons, kisses him.

The true lovers, Angelica and Valentine (Pamela Brown and John Gielgud), regard each other with high esteem, which offsets some of Congreve's cynicism about love in general. When Angelica discovers that Valentine is willing to sacrifice his inheritance because of love, she saves his fortune and they are united.

When he asks to be shown where her bedroom is, she says, "No, I'll run there and hide behind the curtains."

Prue: "I'll hold the door. You shall push me down before you come in." Tattle: "I'll push you down afterwards."

A few seconds later, Prue's nurse enters the bedroom. Out they rush. And poor Mr. Tattle has lost his shoe.

Love for Love

Restoration comedy gave Englishmen a hard, honest look at their own gilded society. Its bawdiness came naturally after Cromwell's Puritans had closed theatres in 1642 and ordered all actors "to be punished as Rogues." When the throne was "restored" to easy-going Charles II, the drama fizzed forth again with exaggerated freedom. *Love for Love*, written by Congreve in 1695 and revived by John Gielgud in 1947, deals mainly with a witty buck who avoids being disinherited and wins a belle. Some strictly secondary fun-lovers are seen atop these pages.

Shameless Mrs. Foresight openly dallies with Mr. Scandal, while her aging husband frets about his health in a mirror.

The Rivals

In Richard Sheridan's plays, most of the Restoration bawdiness has ended, but the comedy lingers on. In *The Rivals,* Lydia Languish loves a youth who tells her he is "half-pay" Ensign Beverly. He is really Captain Absolute, heir to a fortune. Romantic Lydia counted on family opposition and a thrilling elopement, but instead true love runs smoothly. A 1942 Broadway revival had Bobby Clark the bumpkin, Bob Acres, and Mary Boland as the world's most reckless philologist, Mrs. Malaprop.

Acres (Bobby Clark), bent on sprucing up, tell his friend Absolute his "side curls are a little restive."

Captain Absolute and Lydia are happy. She thinks he is an obscure ensign; he thinks she is God's masterpiece.

In the comic duel Acres is relieved to find that Beverly is really his friend Absolute, and all ends happily. The lady at left is famous Mrs. Malaprop.

Acres tussles playfully with Absolute over a slip of paper which challenges Beverly to a duel with Acres.

The School for Scandal

Sheridan's comic masterpiece dissected the backbiters, squabblers and hypocrites of 18th century England. Revived again and again, it had a unique theatre-in-the-round production in Hollywood in 1951. Bosomy Marie Wilson played Lady Teazle, who bickers relentlessly with her elderly husband but resists all attempts by his younger "friends" to lead her astray.

Lady Teazle's fan momentarily holds the audience's eyes as she leans forward to pick it off an 18th century table.

While Joseph Surface tries in vain to seduce her, she stoops again—this time more decorously—to retrieve her fan.

In the 1946 London production Isabel Jeans played clever Mrs. Erlynn (seated, right), who is finally accepted by society. Later when her daughter leaves a fan at Lord Darlington's home, Mrs. Erlynn claims that she herself left the fan and saves her daughter's marriage.

On Broadway in 1947 Cornelia Otis Skinner shone as Mrs. Erlynn. Cecil Beaton (right), who designed the sumptuous settings for both productions, played a London dandy. He also photographed the other two pictures on these pages.

Lady Windermere's Fan

Written in 1892, *Lady Windermere's Fan* is not strictly a comedy. But it is Oscar Wilde's comic rather than his dramatic genius which gives it some vitality. It all has to do with Lord Windermere who is secretly seeing and supporting his young wife's mother, Mrs. Erlynn, who has been too casual morally to enter London society. Her lovely daughter, Lady Windermere, believes her mother is long dead, so when she hears gossip about her husband's secret visits to a woman, the poor girl suspects the worst and feels justified in having a flirtation with sympathetic Lord Darlington. Mother love, a fan, and some fast talk save the day.

In London Dorothy Hyson personified Britain's queenly grace in the role of Lady Windermere.

The Importance of

In the play's nonsensical climax, Ernest shows a valise in which he was abandoned as a baby. An old nurse identifies the valise, proving that Ernest is an aristocrat's son, fit to wed the heroine.

Being Earnest

In 1949 New York had a Wilde revival when *The Importance of Being Earnest*, Oscar Wilde's best comedy, opened on Broadway while his second-best play *Lady Windermere's Fan* was still enjoying a successful run. Directed with great high-comedy style by John Gielgud and acted by an all-English cast which adroitly made the most of Wilde's epigrams, *Earnest* got a warmer welcome than any comedy of that season. Wilde's new popularity stemmed not merely from his wit, but from a new appreciation of his talents. He was a critic of morals who, in pointing out the social hypocrisies of his day, created a world at once lighthearted and deadly.

John Gielgud, who directed Wilde's comedy, also acted its dandified hero who concerned himself with love and cucumber sandwiches.

Lady Bracknell (Margaret Rutherford) squelches the engagement of her daughter (Pamela Brown) by saying, "An engagement should come on a young girl as a surprise, pleasant or unpleasant . . . It is hardly a matter that she should be allowed to arrange for herself."

Valentine, a debonaire and struggling dentist, has just pulled a tooth for Clandon, his rich and touchy landlord.

The waiter, a genius at tact and timely intervention, advises the Clandon twins on how to cope with their newfound papa.

You Never Can Tell

At the family's first and tiffy meal, an elderly solicitor and the waiter try to pour oil as Father deplores the lack of filial respect.

The fun in Shaw's seaside picnic begins when the three untrammeled children of progressive Mrs. Clandon after 18 years meet their conservative father. Watching this eternal battle of the generations is a philosophical old waiter and an intellectual young dentist who finds his wooing of brainy Miss Gloria Clandon harder than pulling teeth. Most recently produced in 1949 by New York's Theatre Guild, this 1897 play has been called "the best farce that has been seen on the English-speaking stage in many years."

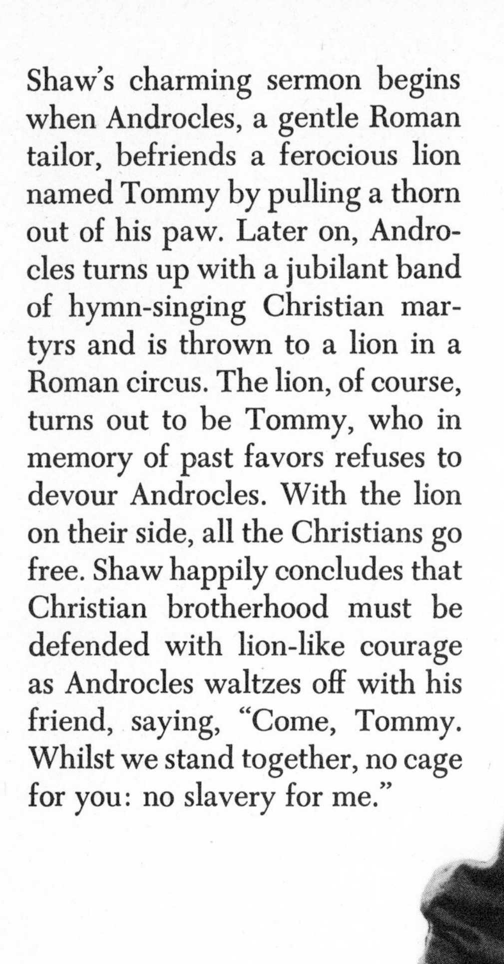

Shaw's charming sermon begins when Androcles, a gentle Roman tailor, befriends a ferocious lion named Tommy by pulling a thorn out of his paw. Later on, Androcles turns up with a jubilant band of hymn-singing Christian martyrs and is thrown to a lion in a Roman circus. The lion, of course, turns out to be Tommy, who in memory of past favors refuses to devour Androcles. With the lion on their side, all the Christians go free. Shaw happily concludes that Christian brotherhood must be defended with lion-like courage as Androcles waltzes off with his friend, saying, "Come, Tommy. Whilst we stand together, no cage for you: no slavery for me."

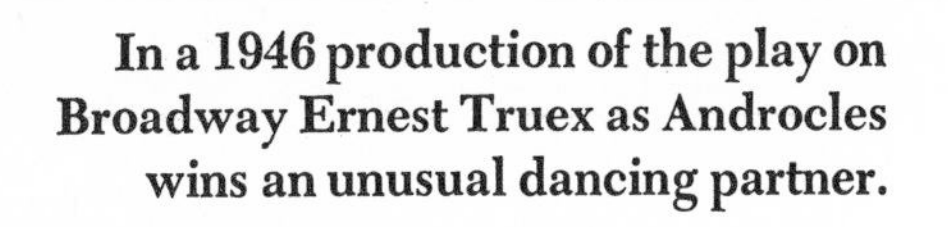

In a 1946 production of the play on Broadway Ernest Truex as Androcles wins an unusual dancing partner.

Androcles and the Lion

While Louis (Bramwell Fletcher) paints his wife Jennifer, she begs him to borrow money from her at any time. Though a scoundrel, he makes her supremely happy.

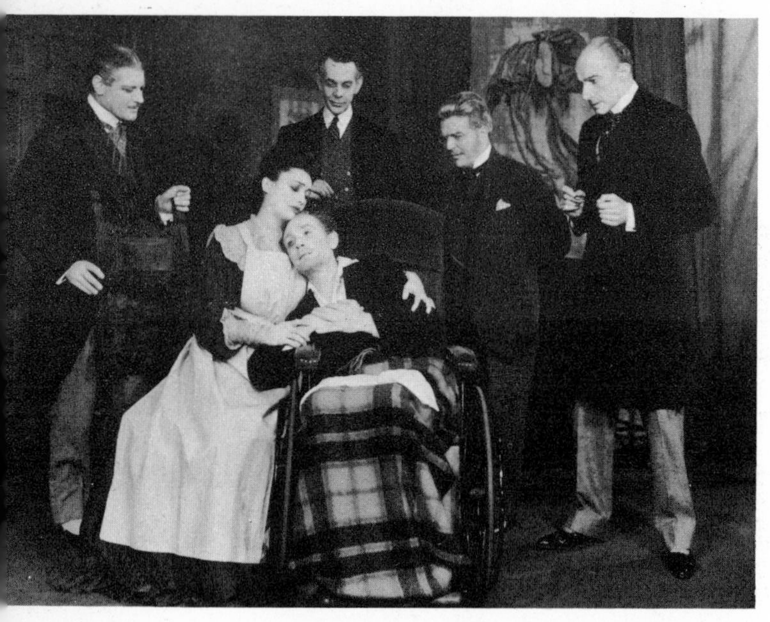

Louis dies, stating his credo, "I believe in Michelangelo, Velasquez and Rembrandt: in the might of the design . . . the redemption of all things by Beauty."

Ridgeon, who let Louis die and has secretly loved his wife, is lost when she says she has just remarried, "People who have married happily once, always marry again."

Jennifer brings her husband to a dinner of doctors who are impressed by his genius, but discover that, unknown to his wife, he is a thief and bigamist. The dilemma: is it better to cure an amoral genius or a commonplace honest man?

The

Candida

Candida is attracted by the adoring poet Marchbanks.

Doctor's Dilemma

In *The Doctor's Dilemma,* written in 1906, Cornell again shone as one of Shaw's benign, slightly unreal heroines. This time she mothers a painter named Louis Dubedat—an amoral, tubercular genius, who is allowed to die by Ridgeon, a moralistic doctor with only a limited amount of a life-saving medicine to dispense. But Dubedat's spirit triumphs in the end.

Shaw's *Candida,* written in 1897, found its best interpreter in Katharine Cornell. Her 1942 revival had Burgess Meredith as the weak and child-like poet who idolized her, and Raymond Massey as her stalwart husband, Reverend Morell.

er strong husband is jealous of the fragile artist.

Candida gives her love to the man who needs her most.

Katharine Hepburn as a fiery heiress laces into one of her admirers (Cyril Richard) for insulting her father, who left her 30 million pounds.

The Millionairess

Shaw's talky comedy *The Millionairess,* written when he was 80, never had a big professional production before 1950 when Katharine Hepburn hurled herself into it like a hurricane. As Epifania, the world's richest girl, who illustrates both the bane and boon of wealth, she cajoled or browbeat three admirers, practiced jiujitsu, and broke chairs as easily as she broke lovers' hearts.

While his mother curses him, and his cousin and nitwit brother gape, Dick Dudgeon (Maurice Evans) boasts he is the Devil's Disciple.

Dick, posing as a parson accused of treason, is tried before General Burgoyne (Dennis King) and the parson's grateful wife (Marcia Hunt).

The Devil's Disciple, produced on Broadway in 1950, centers around the only American ever to be a hero of a full-length Shaw play. He is gallant Dick Dudgeon of Revolutionary War times, who calls himself the devil's disciple to spoof the bogus piety of his Puritan mother. Shaw, who never tired of pointing out that the devil is more enlightened than most God-fearing folk, arranges for Dick to impersonate a good parson whom the British want to hang for treason. Then devilish Dick saves the man of God from the gallows.

The Devil's Disciple

Still posing as the doomed man, Dick is nearly hanged, but is saved by the parson himself. Thus Dick wins freedom and almost wins the parson's wife.

Barry Jones (center) acted with marvelous aplomb the role of an amorous underwear manufacturer, surrounded by extraordinary relatives, friends, and intruders.

Misalliance

Written in 1909-10, Shaw's *Misalliance* was never played much because producers felt it was too talky. Talky indeed it is, but almost all of it is brilliant. The talk takes off from the ostensible theme of the play, which is the projected marriage between a lord's son and an underwear manufacturer's daughter, and goes on to cover a typical Shaw catalogue: parenthood, Socialism, sex, British hypocrisy, masculine hypocrisy, and what duchesses think about modern plumbing. On top of the talk, Shaw added an unexpected dash of slapstick. *Misalliance* was beautifully acted and produced on Broadway in 1952 and, to everybody's surprise, was a hit.

Caesar and Cleopatra

In 1951 an outstanding event in 20th century theatre was the performing by Sir Laurence Olivier and his wife, Vivien Leigh, of two plays delineating the loves of Queen Cleopatra. They were Shaw's comedy, *Caesar and Cleopatra,* and Shakespeare's tragedy, *Antony and Cleopatra.* Given at alternate performances in London and on Broadway, they comprised a girlhood-to-death epic with Leigh as Cleopatra and Olivier doubling as the two Romans who made her, successively, a queen and a woman. The plays, different as they were, fitted curiously well together as if Shaw had written a kind of curtain-raiser to Shakespeare.

Antony and Cleopatra

In Shakespeare, Cleopatra makes Antony so far forget his military duties that he is finally vanquished by his foes.

In Shaw, Caesar makes Cleopatra remember her duties as a 16-year-old queen, telling her to display pride, courage, majesty.

In Shaw's comedy Vivien Leigh, as the child queen, prattles to a middle-aged Caesar (Laurence Olivier) beneath her pet sphinx.

In Shakespeare's tragedy the queen, 18 years later, enacts another fateful scene by the same sphinx as her lover Antony dies at her feet.

Hiding from the conquering Romans in the shadow of a sphinx Cleopatra spies the great Caesar himself, thinks he is just a nice old man.

Caesar and Cleopatra

An earlier Broadway production (1950) of Shaw's *Caesar and Cleopatra* is shown here in greater detail. Caesar was played by Sir Cedric Hardwicke, and the little girl whom he teaches to be a queen was Lilli Palmer. The first thing she learns from Caesar (who visited Egypt in 48 B.C.) is not to cringe. He counsels her to be regal but humane, outspoken but considerate. He warns her that vengeance only leads to more vengeance: "And so, to the end of history, murder shall breed murder, always in the name of right and honor and peace, until the gods are tired of blood and create a race that can understand."

At the end Caesar, knowing he is too old to be her lover, returns to Rome, promising to send her handsome young Mark Antony. The tragic sequel of their love Shaw left, not too confidently, in the hands of Shakespeare.

Still concealing his identity, Caesar leads Cleopatra back to her palace where he teaches her to outshout her bullying old nurse.

Caesar upbraids Cleopatra for her senseless blood-thirstiness when she has assassinated one of Caesar's own enemies. Always her best friend and severest critic, he leaves her in the end, a wiser and stronger queen.

In a flurry of scarves,
Cleopatra is unrolled from a rug
in which she has tried to smuggle
herself into the presence of Caesar
(standing left).

Cleopatra, in her boudoir, follows Caesar's
advice not to squelch her minions:
"Let your women talk,
and you will learn something from them."

A boa constrictor is what Tanner (Maurice Evans) says he is reminded of when Ann Whiteside (Frances Rowe) ensnares him, first with her feather bow and then with her arms.

Ann traps Tanner into marrying her by announcing that she has promised to wed him and then pretending to swoon at his feet. Realizing he might as well give in, he orates, "I solemnly say that I am not a happy man . . . what we have both done is to renounce freedom, renounce tranquillity, above all, renounce the romantic possibilities of an unknown future for the cares of a household and a family."

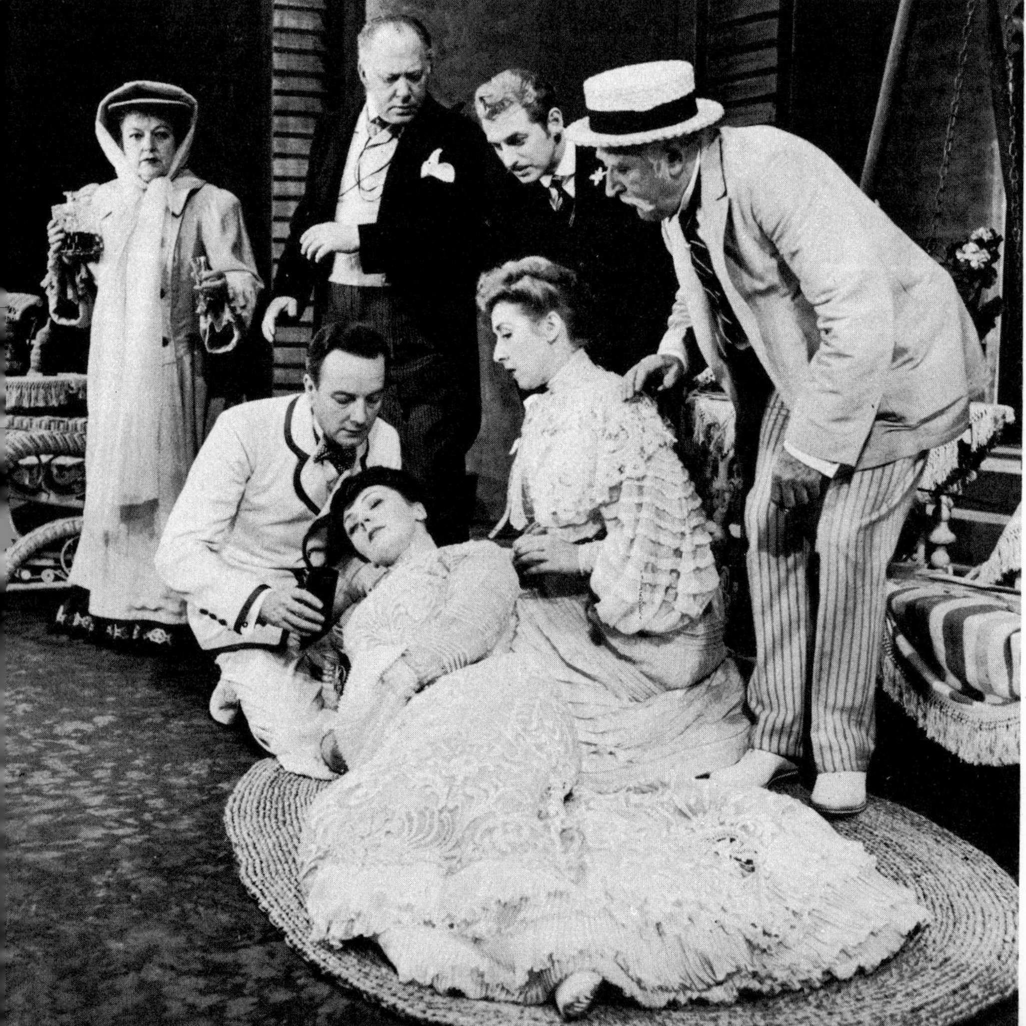

Act III of Shaw's comedy is a two-hour interlude, known as *Don Juan in Hell*, which is omitted in most productions. In 1951 Charles Laughton (below) took it on a triumphant nationwide tour with three other stars, and no scenery or costumes. Laughton acted the Devil.

Man and Superman

In Shaw's wittiest, wordiest comedy, presented on Broadway in 1947, he chose to write about John Tanner, a modern Don Juan who has outgrown his passion for philandering and acquired a moral passion for bettering the world. While Tanner talks and talks about sex, motherhood, democracy and the working man, he tries with high intellectual detachment to resist the charms of a handsome lady who wants him to be the father of her children. He does not resist her long.

Don Juan in Hell, **with scenery and costumes, was charmingly presented in 1948 by London's Arts Theatre Club. Left to right: Don Juan, the Statue, Devil, Donna Anna.**

Sir Cedric Hardwicke as the Statue complains that Heaven is full of Englishmen who are only there because they think they owe it to their position.

Agnes Moorehead as Donna Anna expresses surprise because she feels no pain in Hell, leading Don Juan to say that this proves she was meant to live there.

Charles Boyer as Don Juan serves as Shaw's mouthpiece, voicing his hatred of convention and hypocrisy and his final paradoxical faith in mankind.

Eliza's father (Melville Cooper) shows up to extort five pounds from Professsor Higgens. He finds Eliza wearing a borrowed kimono while her dirty clothes are being burned.

Pygmalion

At her first tea party (below) in the home of Higgens' mother, Eliza in her new white dress tries to talk like a lady. She runs off the track when she begins to chatter about her mother's love of gin, but on the whole she is a hit.

Shaw took his title from the Latin poet Ovid, who told how a sculptor named Pygmalion created a beautiful statue and then fell in love with it. Shaw's Pygmalion is a London professor of phonetics, Henry Higgens, who picks up a poor cockney flower girl, Eliza Doolittle, and by teaching her to speak like a lady transforms her from rags to respectability.

The 1948 Broadway production had Gertrude Lawrence as Eliza, who gets to the heart of the play when she remarks, "You see, really and truly, apart from the things anyone can pick up (the dressing and the proper way of speaking, and so on), the difference between a lady and a flower girl is not how she behaves, but how she is treated."

Fully transformed into a lady, Eliza is hurt because Higgens (Raymond Massey) loses interest in her. But here, after she declares her independence and says she will teach phonetics herself, his interest revives.

Charley's Aunt

Charley's Aunt, by Brandon Thomas, was first given in London in 1892, has outrun any other play three to one. On Broadway in 1940 it was directed by Joshua Logan, had José Ferrer as the Oxford lad who dresses up as an old lady to chaperone his classmate's girlfriends.

Charley's Aunt (José Ferrer) gets a disciplinary poke from behind with a broomstick when she gets too chummy with the boys' girlfriends. As the plot wears on, Auntie gets an ardent suitor, Mr. Spettigue, whom she tries to discourage by pouring tea in his hat. Later when her garter falls down, it is spied by Mr. Spettigue who thinks it is his and snaps it to his own leg. Before the chase ends, Auntie climbs a tree to elude Spettigue, and her friends try to lure her down with brandy.

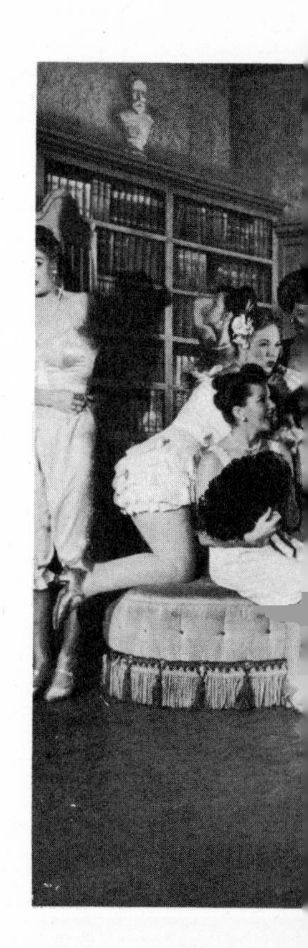

Where's Charley

In 1948 the immortal Aunt turned up as a Broadway musical, with entrancing songs by Frank Loesser and great dancing by Ray Bolger, whom you see gallivanting over this page. The old farce was even more fun now, possibly because Auntie had so many pretty showgirls to ogle.

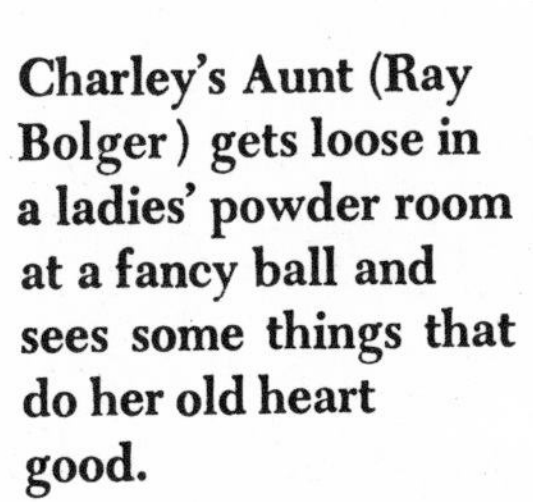

Charley's Aunt (Ray Bolger) gets loose in a ladies' powder room at a fancy ball and sees some things that do her old heart good.

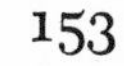

The pub-keeper's pretty daughter, Pegeen (Beatrice Straight) is so dazzled by Christy Mahon because he slew his father "with the help of God," that she even admires his soiled, blistered "little feet."

The Playboy of the Western World

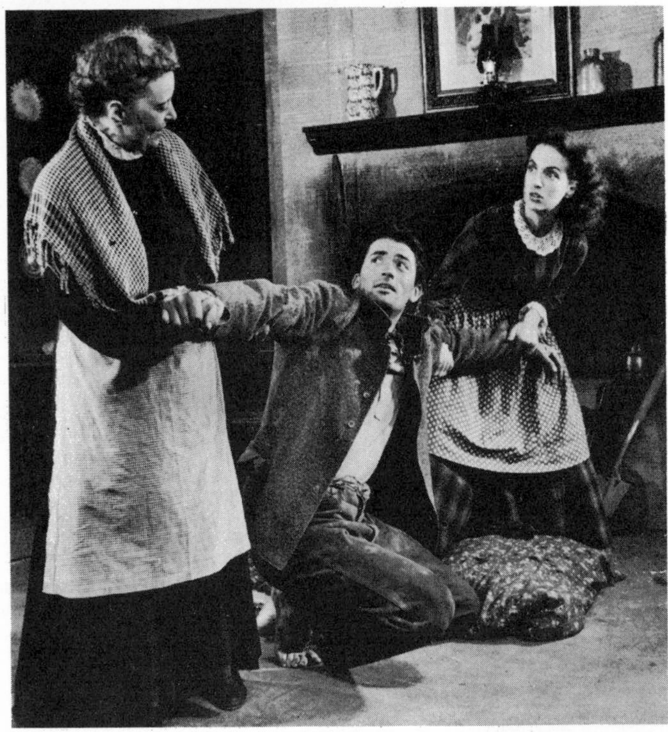

The Widow Quin (June Walker) tries to pull the hero to her cottage because he is a kindred soul. But she only slew her father by hitting him with a rusty pick, which Pegeen calls "sneaky kind of murder."

"A grand story—he tells it lovely," say the neighbors when Christy explains he killed his father with a scythe because he wanted him to wed the Widow Casey, "a walking terror from beyond the hills."

Christy's father who was only bruised, walks in, and again Christy rises up and beats him. But this time the silly villagers turn against their dear playboy.

Four village beauties pay homage to Christy. When he boldly admits his crime, one of them cries, "Then my thousand welcomes," and offers him "a brace of real rich ducks' eggs."

A gem of Irish comedy, J. M. Synge's *The Playboy of the Western World,* incited riots at its 1907 Dublin opening because it twitted the Irish character. Its hero, Christy Mahon, became a village idol when he boasted he had slain his bossy father in a far-off potato patch—a romantic crime that enchanted the villagers. But later when face to face they saw Christy commit what looked like plain unromantic murder, they wanted to hang him.

These 1946 pictures taken at Dennis, Mass., show Gregory Peck having a successful summer fling as Christy.

After almost slaying his father a second time, Christy gets disguised to dodge the villagers' ire. After a final row, he departs, no longer a hero but with his self-respect.

Helen Hayes (opposite) acts a young mother who returns to her children after years in India. Her daughter, Amy (Mary MacArthur, right), and chum (Bethel Leslie) imagine mother is planning a sinful meeting with young Steve.

Alice Sit-by-the-Fire

A skillful writer of comedy, J. M. Barrie seemed bent on proving to a Victorian world that the theatre could be as genteel as a vicarage tea party. But despite his embarrassing fits of sugariness, Barrie had a strong sense of humanity and contributed to the ever-fascinating spectacle of Englishmen becoming civilized. His *Alice-Sit-by-the-Fire*, an exercise in pure charm produced first in 1905, had a successful summer revival in 1946 at Bucks County, Pa., with both Helen Hayes and her daughter, Mary, giving delightful performances.

In his bachelor's flat Steve (Donald Murphy) shares his chops with a half-starved slavey (Patricia Kirkland). It is here that Amy comes to save her happily married mother from having an imagined affair with Steve.

For a happy ending the mother allows Amy to believe she has arranged a reconciliation between her and her husband (John Williams). To save her children from any more such wild notions, the mother resolves to be Alice-sit-by-the-fire.

Exultant after a major political triumph, John Shand (Richard Waring) is hailed by his cheering constituents and the adoring Maggie.

Though John forgets their second wedding anniversary, Maggie's three brothers do not. Journeying down from Scotland for the day, they give her a fine, expensive shawl and take considerable pride in their extravagance.

What Every Woman Knows

With a steadfast eye on a seat in Parliament and a high place in his own party, John Shand thunders along his political way, never once suspecting his rise is due to anything but his own genius. His wife, Maggie . . . an underestimated woman . . . works quietly with love and loyalty to preserve this delusion and, at the same time, to make him the man he thinks he is. June Duprez starred as Maggie in this 1946 Repertory Theatre production of the Barrie classic.

John's career is suffering a serious recession when Maggie saves the day by skillfully re-writing a crucial speech. Confronted with the awful knowledge that a woman can make her husband's success . . . as every woman knows . . . John experiences a profound inner struggle before he can accept this fact and Maggie.

John's masculine roughness temporarily fascinates the refined Lady Sybil (Mary Alice Moore) and John, in turn, is dazzled by her elegance. Here he bestows on her a ruby pendant and a promise of undying love. Maggie, at right, for reasons of her own. does not interrupt the tender scene.

In *Blithe Spirit*, Coward's best comedy, Charles Condomine (Clifton Webb) meets the ghost of his dead wife, Elvira (Leonora Corbett).

Elvira, who is invisible to all but Charles, raises hell by tormenting Charles' second wife and making a maid drop a teatray.

Noel Coward

Coward's gossamer talents as playwright, composer, lyricist, actor, and film-maker are easy to deprecate, but they remain a remarkable theatre phenomenon. His comedies, at their best, are expertly inconsequential. But, surprisingly, he will be longest remembered for three or four romantic songs.

Gertrude Lawrence and Coward hammed hilariously as a smalltime music-hall team in his playlet *Red Peppers*.

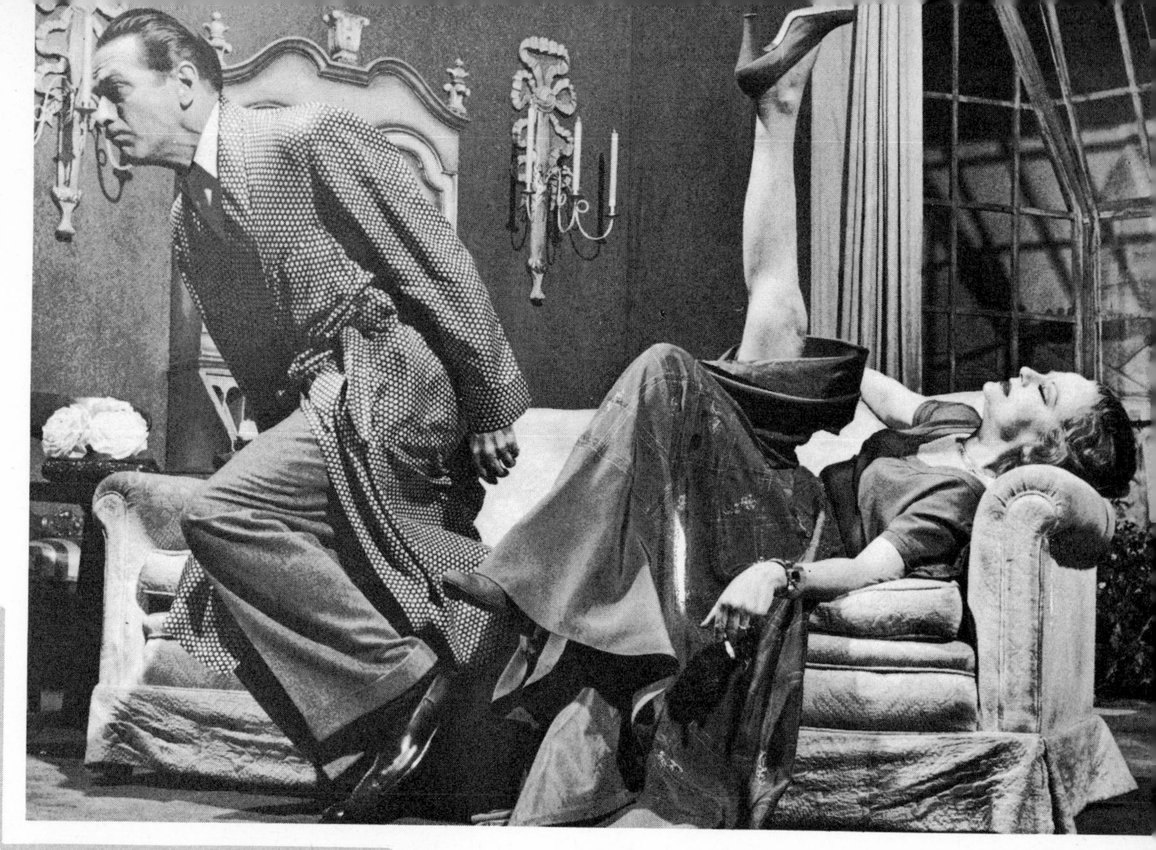

Private Lives, in which a giddy pair get hitched, unhitched, and rehitched, was revived in 1947 with Tallulah Bankhead and Donald Cook indulging in no end of chic horseplay.

At the end, Charles' second wife (Peggy Wood) dies and also becomes a ghost, whom he tries to expel through a medium (Mildred Natwick).

Happily freed from two bickering ghosts, Charles tells them off before taking a long, long trip. They can answer only by breaking vases.

Quadrille

At left are scenes from Noel Coward's *Quadrille,* a 1952 London hit which offered the durable glamor of the Lunts in the elegance of Cecil Beaton settings. Lunt acted a U.S. railroad tycoon and Fontanne was an English lady. Each of them has made a regrettable marriage to somebody else. At top, their respective spouses have fallen in love and, meeting in a railroad café, are running off together. In the middle, the runaways are caught embracing by Lunt and Fontanne, who politely turn away. At bottom, the jilted ones have fallen in love with each other and, in the same café, are leaving their unworthy mates forever.

After a busy day with wartime worries, Cabinet Minister Sir John is soothed by his mistress, Olivia.

Olivia's son invites Sir John's wife to his home in hopes she will reclaim her husband and end his mother's liaison. But the giddy wife refuses to live with John.

O Mistress Mine

Terence Rattigan, who is best at serious drama, nevertheless wrote a diverting comedy for the Lunts, *O Mistress Mine*. Its widowed heroine, Olivia, is the mistress of a wartime cabinet minister in charge of producing tanks. He cannot wed her because the scandal of a divorce from his flamboyant wife might impede the war effort. All goes well until Olivia's priggish 17-year-old son returns from Canada and tries to "reform" his mother. With this comedy the Lunts cheered up London in 1944, Broadway in 1946.

Wearing an apron to help Olivia wash dishes, John finally wins her son's esteem by advising him how to capture a girlfriend. And the old folks peacefully live on in sin.

The Cocktail

T. S. Eliot chats backstage with Director Martin Browne and Actress Irene Worth at the world premiere of "The Cocktail Party" at the 1949 Edinburgh festival. Scenery is inscribed with "CHAMPAGNE" from an earlier Sherek production.

Party

To the cocktail party of Edward Chamberlayne comes a mysterious guest (Alec Guiness, left)—a sort of priestly psychiatrist, who gives advice to troubled mortals.

The Cocktail Party, Nobel prize-winning poet T. S. Eliot's unexpectedly popular experiment in dramatic verse was successful both in London and on Broadway. Behind a façade of high-comedy satire the poet explored a profound theme: that most human beings are unfit for a life of service and sacrifice to God and can find Christian salvation only through a tolerant acceptance of each others' weaknesses.

Now in his office the soul-doctor advises Mrs. Chamberlayne and her husband, who have been estranged, to resume their life together and diligently make the best of a bad job.

Celia, who has had a loveless liaison with Chamberlayne, is told by the doctor that she is one of those rare and lonely souls capable of a truly Christian life.

Thomas: "Laughter is surely the surest touch of genius . . . an irrelevancy which almost amounts to revelation."

Chaplain, Mayor, and Judge blandly leave the young lovers locked in the cellar.

After worsting a sly seducer, Thomas says to Jennet: "You force me to tell you the disastrous truth. I love you."

Christopher Fry's dramatic powers are faulty, but he has written, here and there, better stage poetry than anyone since Shakespeare or Jonson. This medieval comedy hinges on the unexplained disappearance of Skipps the junk-dealer. The lovely Jennet does not want to be burned as a witch for turning Skipps into a dog. But life-weary young Thomas wants to be hung for killing Skipps. By the time Skipps strolls in, Thomas and Jennet, acted by John Gielgud and Pamela Brown, want to go on living and loving together.

Serving lad (Richard Burton) to his lass: "We're lovers in a deep and safe place and never lonely any more."

The Lady's not for Burning

Jennet cries: "Am I to go to the flames at noon? Why must they brand themselves with me!"

The four colonels wait to be led by the Wicked Fairy (Rex Harrison) to inspect the Sleeping Beauty.

The Love of Four Colonels

Waiting below for a kiss is the fairy-tale heroine of *The Love of Four Colonels* by Peter Ustinov, England's cleverest young actor-playwright. His play had Lilli Palmer and Rex Harrison each acting five roles in a series of charade-like scenes. They told how each of four officers from four countries revealed his national foibles by his method of wooing the Sleeping Beauty. A London hit for two years, the *Colonels* amused Broadway in 1952.

The beauty (Lilli Palmer) wakes up in turn for each colonel, and becomes briefly his ideal woman.

Broadway

An outstanding virtue of the American theatre has been the variety of its offerings and its hospitality to new ideas. Broadway, in its short history as a theatrical center, has been, heaven knows, a cheap and gaudy street. But it has also been a wide and roomy street. And, like America itself, it has played host to talent and genius from many lands and many ages.

At the turn of the century the theatre was dominated by its great producers – the Belascos and Frohmans and Erlangers, and by its great actors who trouped across the country almost as indefatigably as the early settlers. Later the playwrights took on prominence; variety and resourcefulness is their only common characteristic. Eugene O'Neill drew inspiration from the Greeks, the early Christians, the Orientals, and Harry Hope's waterfront saloon. Philip Barry see-sawed between high comedy and mysticism. Sidney Howard turned from realistic drama to fantasy. Others, such as Hellman, Kelly, Odets, Miller, Williams, Saroyan, and Inge, developed a clearly individual accent. American drama eludes summarizing except in a few respects: it is short on wit —S. N. Behrman stands almost alone as a writer of consistently polished comedy, and it is short on the power for which the theatre was first created—the power to exalt and inspire. Artists and visionaries such as Gordon Craig and Robert Edmond Jones have a hard time in the theatre, but the theatre needs them badly.

American playwrights, to their great credit, do not wear blinders. Looking sideways right and left, they see social problems, human foibles, odd corners and byways. But they still wear visors, which handicaps their looking up.

FOOTNOTES OF A PLAY-GOER: *Standard of dramatic criticism in New York newspapers:* highest in the world. *Power of critics:* greater than they themselves desire, but not a serious problem. *Playhouses:* uncomfortable, dull, and often too big, but slowly improving. *First night audiences:* more intelligent than they look. *Acting:* generally better than the plays. *Scenery:* thanks to designers like Mielziner, Oenslager, and Aronson, very good. But these men seldom have a chance to venture radically. *Young playwrights:* too few. *Old playwrights:* too few. *Young composers:* too few. *Musical shows:* fine, but not enough original books. *Theatre prices:* very reasonable, considering other rising costs. *Theatre versus TV and movies:* silly subject. *Comedies:* not enough good ones. *Foreign importations:* not enough good ones. *Repertory theatres:* an idle dream. *Audiences:* lovely people, but not representative enough of the entire population. *Off-Broadway theatre:* more power to it—it needs it. *University and civic theatres:* often excellent. *Future of Broadway:* bright.

CIGARETTES

Anna discovers true love in the form of a shipwrecked sailor (Kevin McCarthy) who is rescued by her father's barge.

Anna Christie

Of all Eugene O'Neill's serious plays, *Anna Christie* has had the most conventional popularity. His first major Broadway hit, it established him in 1921 as a rugged young playwright who seemed to pump real sea air into the theatre ventilating system and could write about human beings—especially low-lifers—with almost religious compassion. O'Neill himself rejected *Anna* because he felt it lacked spiritual significance and once refused to have it printed in a collection of his works. Despite its rather obvious story of an ex-prostitute who finds redemption in her love for a sailor, *Anna* won a Pulitzer Prize and has been given repeatedly all over the world. With one exception, these pictures are from a 1952 revival, which didn't fare too well.

Anna's new life, after her shoddy career, starts in a waterfront dive where she awaits her father and chats with one of his old girl friends. Unaware of Anna's arrival, he is downing a quick one at the bar.

Anna (Celeste Holm) purges her soul by confessing her sinful past to her father and her sweetheart, both of whom finally forgive her.

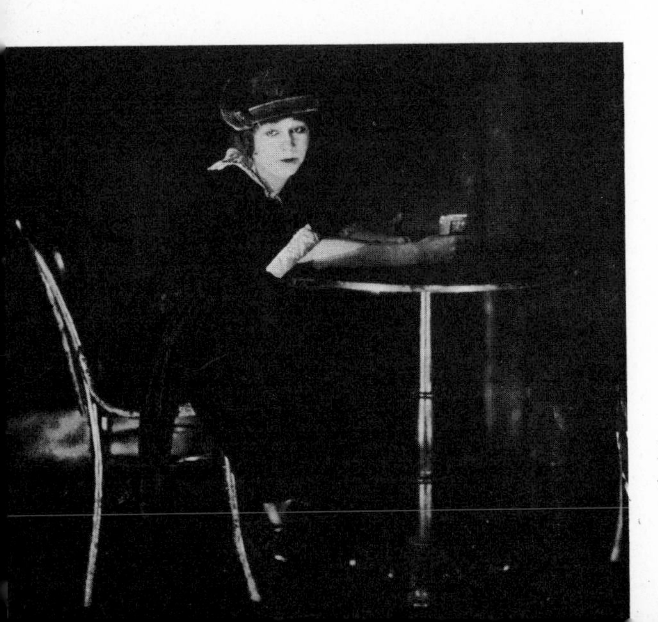

Pauline Lord, the least glamorous of all the Annas, was the best—wistful, brave, and heartbreaking.

Ephraim Cabot (Karl Malden)
takes courage from God
after his wife and son have
tragically betrayed him.

Desire

Under the Elms

His old love for the farmlands is described by Cabot while his young wife Abbie (Carol Stone) dreams of another kind of love.

Her young love for her husband's son Eben (Douglas Watson) blazes up in Abbie as she drags him from his bed, lures him downstairs to woo her.

In his *Desire Under the Elms* Eugene O'Neill proved his awareness of Greek tragedy. For though his characters lack the classic stature, he cast them in the classic mold; they are big enough to love and big enough to suffer. This tragedy was first produced in 1924 and revived in 1952 by ANTA (American National Theatre Academy). Its hero is 76-year-old Ephraim Cabot, a grisly monarch of the soil who keeps his sons subjugated to his bleak New England farmland. For his third wife Ephraim brings home young Abbie, and prides himself that he will make her produce offspring even as he has made his land produce. But Ephraim's will and energy are of no avail when Abbie falls in love with his young son Eben, and the old tyrant must face the tragedy of his failing powers.

Proving her love for Eben, who believes charge that she wanted to disinherit him, Abbie smothers their baby in the crib while Cabot sleeps.

Unaware that Eben is father to Abbie's baby, Cabot fights and taunts Eben, saying that Abbie had the son to keep Eben from inheriting the farm.

Swinging a pickaninny on his arm, De Lawd in heaven with his angels enjoys a fish fry in the happy days before he created mankind.

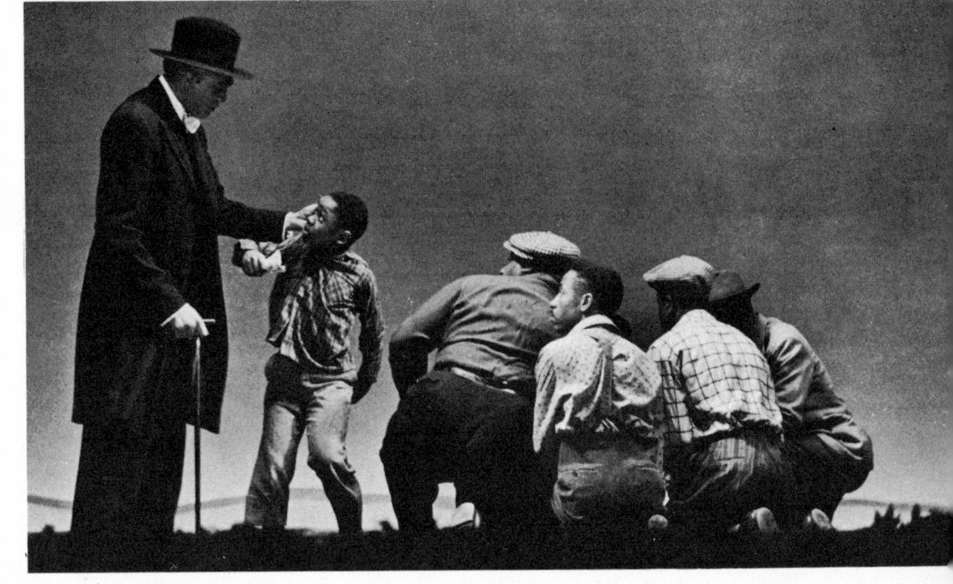

Sunday crapshooters are chided by De Lawd who walks the earth as a country preacher trying to reform big and little backsliders.

After forty days of complete rain the sky brightens and Noah (right) peers through his spyglass for a place to moor.

The Green Pastures

From Roark Bradford's book of Negro Bible tales Marc Connelly wrote *Green Pastures,* a 1930 Pulitzer Prize winner, which is one of the most appealing bits of Americana in the nation's theatre. It consists simply of Old Testament scenes as they might be described by a beatific preacher to his Sunday School. A 1951 revival had Robert Edmond Jones' original sets and another Hall Johnson choir. But for several reasons (for one, it played in a too-big theatre) it drew no audiences.

Noah and his kinfolk stand on the ark as the deluge begins, while skeptical sinners expecting only a trivial drizzle raise their umbrellas

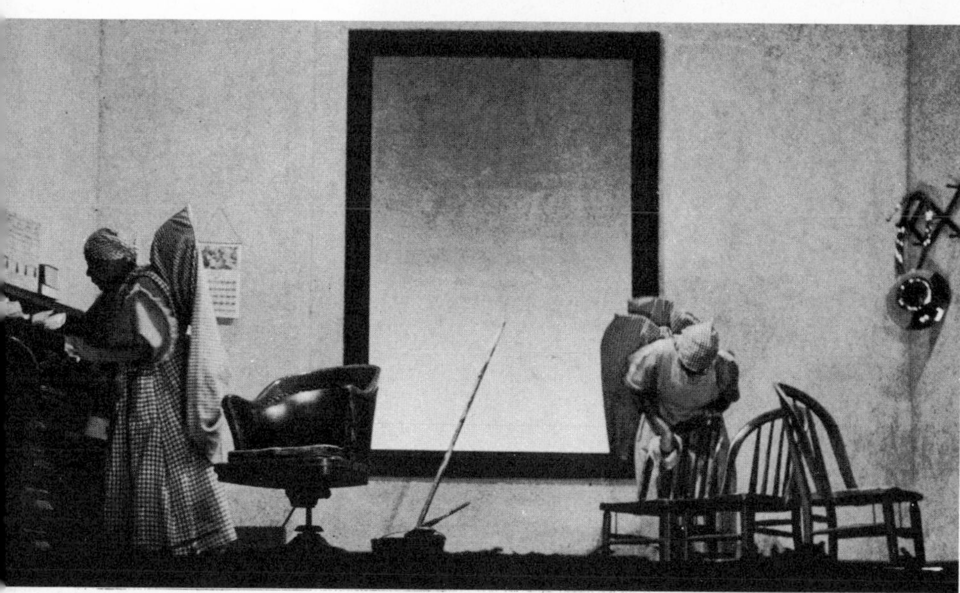

In De Lawd's office in heaven angel mammies tidy up the place, sensibly wearing dusters over their wings. At right hangs Gabriel's horn.

In New Orleans style, the jazzy debauchees of Babylon go their wicked ways despite the warnings of a Jeremiah-like prophet.

Harry (Alfred Lunt) is a vaudeville hoofer who recognizes Irene, the munition king's blond mistress (Lynn Fontanne), as his partner years ago in a cherished one-night romance in an Omaha hotel.

Idiots Delight

Robert Sherwood, a charming writer of comedy, won a 1936 Pulitzer Prize with *Idiot's Delight,* which betokened his widening interest in world problems. Set in an Alpine hotel, his play was a duel between the good people, represented by Harry the American vaudevillian with his troupe, and the bad people, a group of munitions-makers who cynically fomented wars for their own profit.

A 1951 revival of the play by the New York City Theatre Company had Ruth Chatterton as Irene (left) and Lee Tracy as Harry, surrounded by his six chicks.

While Regina Hubbard (Tallulah Bankhead) and her predatory brothers hatch a big business deal, her tippling sister (Patricia Collinge) cringes at their plotting.

The Little Foxes

In 1939 Lillian Hellman's *The Little Foxes* established her as a major U.S. dramatist and a relentless but just assailant of American morals. Tallulah Bankhead was magnificent as the Lady Macbeth of a southern city about the turn of the century. Sister to an avaricious clan of financiers, she schemes with her shady brothers to build a cotton mill, tries to bully her mortally sick husband into joining them, and outwits her own kin at their double-dealing.

At the end, after she has allowed her husband to die of heart failure, Regina queens it over her two brothers and young nephew. She is now the financial ruler of the Hubbard clan.

Our Town

A poetic chronicle of everyday life and death in a New Hampshire village, Thornton Wilder's *Our Town* won a 1938 Pulitzer Prize and is fairly assured of a permanent place in American drama. Like the ancient dramatists, Wilder used a bare stage and employed a commentator somewhat like a Greek chorus leader. If the play lapses occasionally into sentimentality, it nevertheless speaks movingly about human beings and their failure to enjoy each other until it is too late.

Thornton Wilder sometimes acts the commentator when his play is given off-Broadway.

Young love blossoms when the boy and girl (Martha Scott) meet at the village soda fountain, represented only by a plank laid across two chairs.

The philosophical commentator, played by Frank Craven, talks with Emily Webb shortly after her death. Behind her, peaceful in the village graveyard, are other spirits of the deceased.

The lovers study their homework "upstairs" on ladders while their mothers return from choir practice and listen to the town gossip.

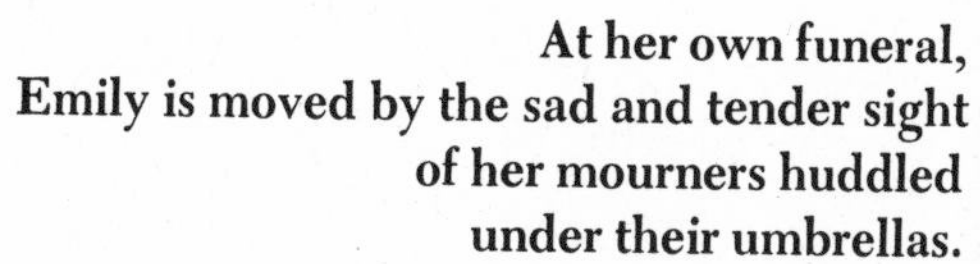

At her own funeral, Emily is moved by the sad and tender sight of her mourners huddled under their umbrellas.

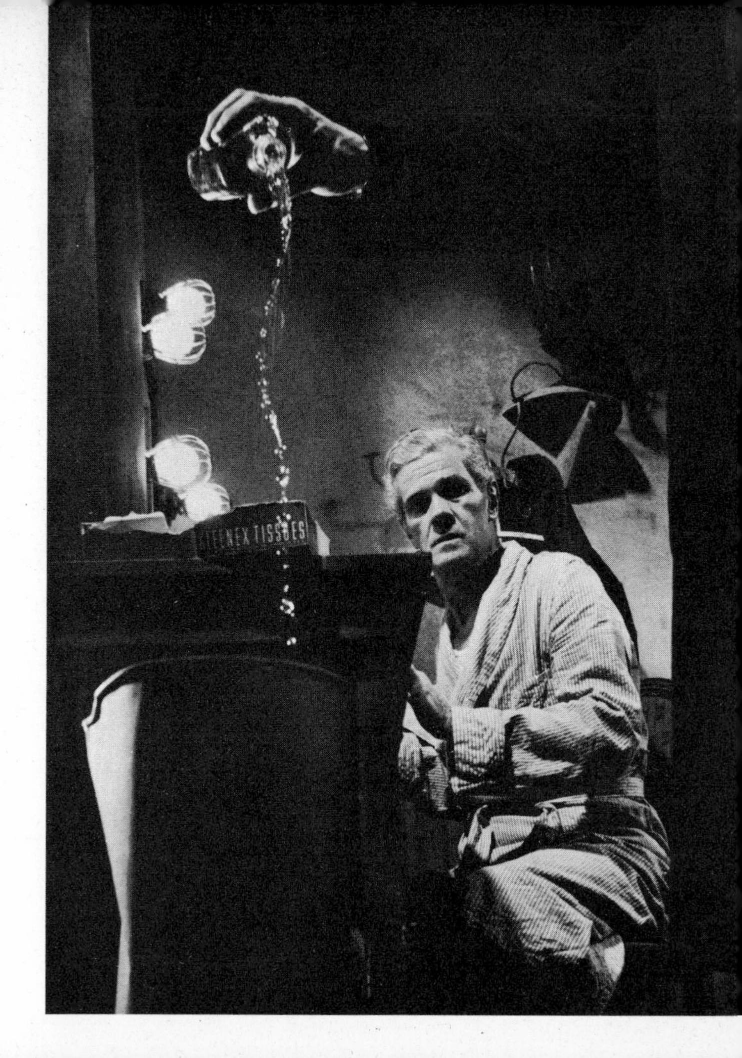

A former stage star (Paul Kelly), trying to fortify his courage for a comeback, watches in horror as a stage manager empties a bottle of alcoholic cough medicine which the actor has been secretly gulping.

In his early plays (*Waiting for Lefty, Awake and Sing*) Clifford Odets was eloquently aware of social problems. In *The Country Girl* (1950) he focused on the personal problems of an alcoholic actor, Frank Elgin, and his long-suffering wife. At first the wife seems a villain who has driven her gifted husband to drink. But as the play unfolds it becomes apparent, in one of the most interesting character reversals in modern drama, that the wife is a loyal and blameless helpmeet.

The Country Girl

After years of being misunderstood, the actor's wife (Uta Hagen) breaks into sobs at his repeated accusations that she has damaged his life.

Angelic slobs seeking truth and happiness in Nick's bar are Kitty the prostitute (Julie Haydon), Harry the dancer (Gene Kelly) and Joe the fixer (Eddie Dowling), who is trying to gladden Kitty with a dancing doll.

The Time of Your Life

In the season of 1939-40 William Saroyan had two plays on Broadway that exemplified his blend of humor, pathos and hokum. *Love's Old Sweet Song* got nowhere, but *The Time of Your Life* as directed and acted by Eddie Dowling won a Pulitzer Prize and justified Brooks Atkinson's statement that it was "a prose poem in ragtime." One of the hardest figures to assess, Saroyan is either too easy to like or too easy to dismiss.

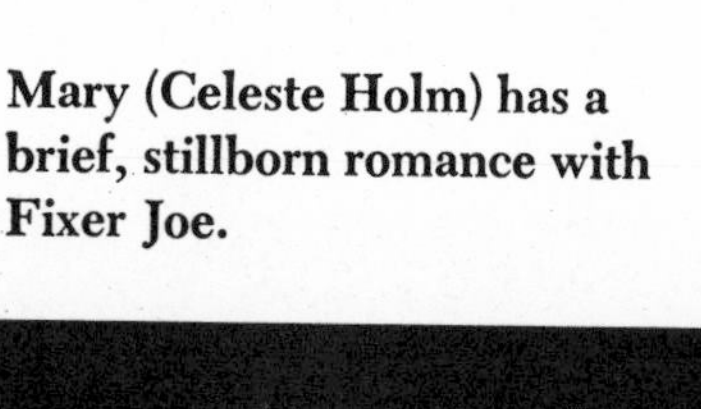

Willie finds joy with a super pinball machine that spells "American Destiny."

Mary (Celeste Holm) has a brief, stillborn romance with Fixer Joe.

Kit Carson, a sublime braggart, shoots a cop who torments Kitty, ends the play.

Whiteside (Moss Hart) and a prankish friend dispose of a film star who is causing an undue amount of trouble by closing her in a mummy case and carting her away.

The Man Who Came to Dinner

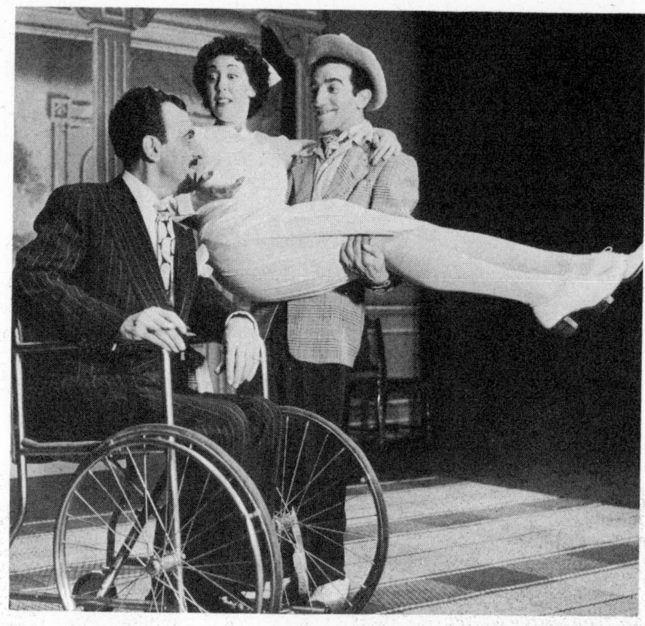

Miss Preen, the great man's nurse, is swept off her feet by one of his wolfish cronies.

A 1939 comedy of manners, as sharp in its way as Molière's *Les Precieuses Ridicules,* is Moss Hart's and George Kaufman's lampoon of high class Bohemia. The hero is Sheridan Whiteside, patterned after the late Alexander Woollcott. He goes on a lecture tour, is invited to dine with an Ohio family, and injures his hip by falling on the ice. For four weeks he settles down as a bossy and bellowing guest, summoning around him a dizzy entourage of stage and screen friends. In 1945 the play made a tour of Army camps—as did so many other Broadway shows—with co-author Moss Hart as the wheelchair tyrant.

Service men at Camp Mitchell, Long Island, had a wonderful time watching the play.

Whiteside browbeats his nurse when she scolds him for devouring candy.

Departing at the end, Whiteside falls and injures his hip again. He is carried back and the reign of terror resumes.

Bigger dangles a rat he killed in the slummy Chicago flat where he lives with his sister (left), brother, and mother, who is a laundress. He becomes a chauffeur to Mrs. Dalton, whose daughter Mary dabbles in Communism, is attracted by the vigorous Bigger.

Bringing Mary Dalton home from a party, Bigger complies with her drunken request that he carrry her to bed. When she tries to seduce him, Bigger accidentally strangles the girl lest she betray his presence to her blind mother.

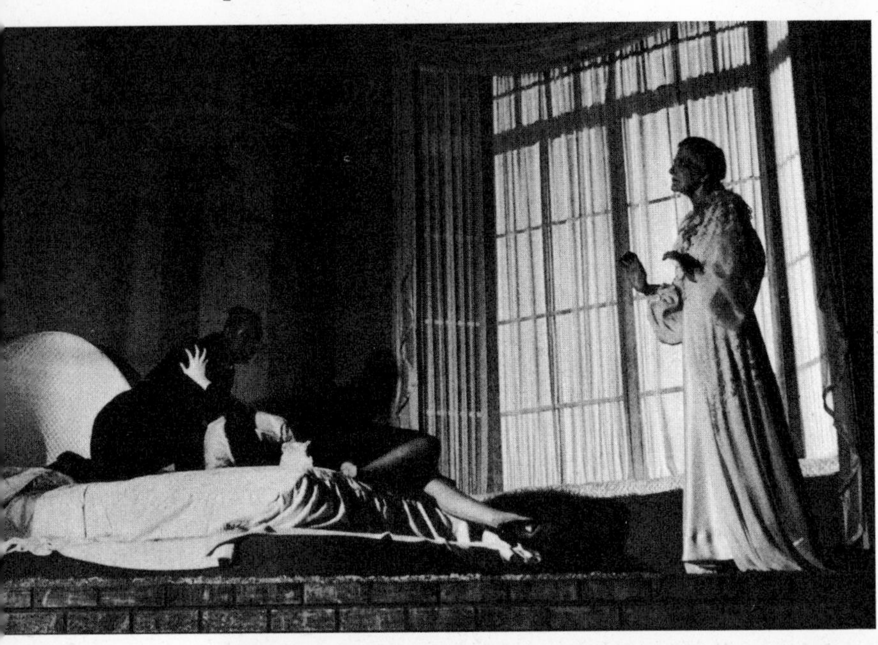

Native Son

From 1930 on, Broadway took a greater interest in social problems and in 1941 came up with an impressive Orson Welles production of *Native Son* by Paul Green and Richard Wright. Canada Lee was outstanding as Bigger Thomas, a confused and rebellious Negro who unwittingly kills a white girl and brings down a torrent of hatred upon his race.

Holding the tragic consequence of his innocent crime, Bigger in a panic decides to stuff her body in a furnace. Traces of it are found and lead to his arrest.

Awaiting execution, Bigger finds some peace by realizing that the race hatred aroused by his trial is not aimed at him alone but is a problem for all mankind to overcome.

The happy Antrobus family (below) includes mother, father, son, daughter, a maid named Lilly Sabina, and a pet dinosaur and mammoth.

After the Ice Age, Mr. Antrobus epitomizes all tired businessmen, attends an Atlantic City convention for honorable mammals, and ogles a cutie who is Lilly.

As the Ice Age comes down, and the townspeople huddle around the Antrobus fireplace, Lilly cries to audience, "Please start handing up your chairs. We'll need everything for this fire. Save the human race."

The great flood hits Atlantic City, and Mr. Antrobus, like Noah, herds his family and all the mammals, two of each, into a boat. The Antrobuses were acted (left to right) by Fredric March, Florence Heflin, Montgomery Clift, Florence Eldridge. Lilly, of course, was Tallulah Bankhead.

After the war Lilly, now as a camp follower, returns to the Antrobus home in Excelsior, N.J., and the family goes on. Says Mrs. Antrobus, "Too many people have suffered and died for us to start reneging now."

The Skin of Our Teeth

The Pulitzer prize-winning Thornton Wilder, who may be the most important playwright the U.S. has had so far, startled Broadway in 1941 with *The Skin of Our Teeth*. Part comedy, part allegory, part nonsense, part serious thinking, the play broke all rules of drama to present a history of man's ability to exist by the skin of his teeth.

The play opens in Deen's corner drugstore in Maxwell, Ga. When a Negro soldier enters (right), one man remarks, "It makes me plum want to puke to see a black coon in a uniform." Not all the white people were so minded.

Strange Fruit

Tracy Deen (Melchor Ferrer), whose family are leading citizens in Maxwell, finds his only love and understanding with the Negro girl Nonnie (Jane White), who bears his child.

At Tracy's funeral his sister receives a humble bouquet from Nonnie, who never tells the Deen family that she is bearing Tracy's child.

In the 1940's, Broadway was especially concerned with Negro problems. One of the most theatrically effective discussions of the subject was *Strange Fruit,* Lillian Smith's dramatization of her novel. It told the story of Tracy Deen, a well-born white man in a small Georgia mill town, and of his love for Nonnie Anderson, an intelligent Negro girl. The strange fruit of their love, which was frustrated by misunderstanding and racial prejudice, was the murder of Deen and the lynching of an innocent Negro.

In a cafe Nonnie's brother Ed (in white suit) hears that Tracy Deen got his sister into trouble. He punches his informant in the jaw, sets out to avenge his sister by killing Tracy.

Ed rushes home, confesses to Nonnie and her sister Bess that he has just killed Tracy. Nonnie gives him money so that he can flee the manhunt which is about to start. Later an innocent Negro is lynched.

The Glass Menagerie

The Glass Menagerie, Tennessee Williams' first Broadway play, won him a 1945 Critics' Circle Prize. Its two sad heroines—mother and daughter—personified the human spirit mired in false dreams and feelings of inferiority but yearning for love and grace. Born in Mississippi, Williams is unquestionably a major theatre talent of the mid-20th century, though he lingers too long perhaps on connubial frustrations in the Southland.

Outside their tenement home, Mother Wingfield calls after son Tom to look for a nice young man. "Find one that's clean-living and doesn't drink—and ask him out for Sister." Snaring a husband for her daughter, who is lame and pitifully shy, is a desperate family problem.

The Gentleman Caller (Anthony Ross) brought home by Tom turns out to be a man whom Laura (Julie Haydon) has secretly loved. He overcomes her shyness and brings her a few romantic moments as they sit together on the floor.

A poignantly comic bit from the play had Laurette Taylor as the Mother trying to earn money by selling magazine subscriptions to friends over the phone. She hopes to entice them by telling the plots of trashy serials that have just started.

Too sick with self-doubt to join the family dinner (below), Laura lies alone while the Caller and Tom (Eddie Dowling) toast the South. Though Laura never wins the Caller, his sympathy gives her more courage to live.

Ida Scott? This is Amanda Wingfield. We missed you at the D.A.R. last Monday.

You haven't renewed your subscription . . . just when that new serial is getting off.

A debutante is thrown off her horse while taking the jumps at the regatta.

Her spine is injured. Yes, that's right, Ida. The horse stepped right on her.

There is only one surgeon who can save her from being paralyzed for life.

He is the man she is engaged to . . . He has the most dreadful weakness. He drinks.

What's burning? Oh, Honey . . . Go take a look in the oven.

And I'll hold the wire . . . What do you know—that woman hung up

A rich junk king, Harry Brock (Paul Douglas) gets shaved and shined in his suite while being interviewed by a magazine writer, Paul Verall. At right is Harry's pet blonde, Billie.

Born Yesterday

A comedy hit in 1949, *Born Yesterday* by Garson Kanin had a high-minded point of view, and behind its sex-appeal and gags was a serious preachment for responsible citizenship. Its heroine, an ex-chorus girl named Billie Dawn, is living in Washington with a junk-dealer who aspires to high-level bribery. Afraid Billie is too dumb for polite society, he hires a young liberal to educate her. After two months of the Pygmalion treatment, Billie becomes a solid citizen, gets wise to her boy-friend, brings about his downfall, and marries her tutor.

Judy Holliday acted Billie, who begins her education by dutifully marking all newspaper items which she cannot understand.

Brock tears up Billie's new books because since he hired Verall to educate her, she refuses to sign crooked business documents on which he needs her name

The Washington Post
WASHINGTON, WEDNESDAY, JANUARY 16, 1946
Single Copy Price 5¢
Nation-Wide Meat Strike Called for Toda
All 45-Point U.S. Soldiers Will Be Discharged by April 3
268,000 Set For Walkout; 200,000 Quit Electric Jobs
Kimmel Says Navy 'Misled' Him on Japs
House Military Group Maps Ultimatum to Labor Committee
Army Demobilization Chart
CUMULATIVE RETURNS TO CIVILIAN LIFE
State of Union Talk Delayed Until Monday
Explosion Kills 12 Miners in West Virginia
Phone Strike Causes Delay In Fighting Md. House Blaze
Truman Repeats Conviction Steel Strike Can Be Averted
U.S. to Keep 'Needed' Islands Japanese Held, Truman Says
AFL Taxi Drivers End Strike In Obedience to Union Order
Troopship Sends Distress Signal
Today's Index

The Iceman

Young Joe is resentful when an old Boer war veteran speaks slightingly of "niggers." But the Hope Saloon patrons, by and large, live peaceably together.

Harry Hope (Dudley Digges) is delighted when all his friends, including three tarts, celebrate his birthday with a cake and presents.

Hickey, the glad-hand salesman (James Barton), is wildly welcomed by most of the saloon customers because he always throws a big party for Harry Hope.

Hickey, with madness in his eyes, confesses he killed his wife for loving him too much, and thus rid her of *her* dream. From here on, his disciples reject him in horror.

Cometh

Eugene O'Neill's last drama was about a remarkable collection of down-and-outers in a 1912 New York saloon. Thanks to their dreams and the generosity of the proprietor, Harry Hope, the derelicts maintain some shreds of self-respect. But when a glib-talking, smilingly sinister salesman named Hickey forces them all to face the truth about himself, they sink into a deathlike stupor. In the end they cast off Hickey's baleful spell and live again.

In a Chicago company, Blanche was effectively played by Uta Hagen. She tore into this scene with panther-like fury when Stanley forces her to stand beneath a bare light bulb, revealing that she is not as young as she pretends to be.

A Streetcar Named Desire

After a fierce quarrel brought about by Blanche's endless meddling, her sister Stella (Kim Hunter) and her husband Stanley (Marlon Brando), are reconciled on the stairway of their ramshackle flat.

Tennessee Williams' second Broadway hit, expertly directed by Elia Kazan, proved that this young member of the nostalgic Southern school could bring a poetic mood to the stage and make it sting like a whip. *Streetcar* is the highly theatrical case history of desperate Blanche DuBois, who hides her maladjusted sexuality beneath a too-ladylike surface. When she goes to visit her sister in New Orleans, Blanche collides tragically with the animal honesty of her sister's husband, Stanley, and is taken away in a straitjacket.

Acting the coquette, Blanche (Jessica Tandy) bows to Mitch (Karl Malden), whom she has lured into courting her. Mitch jilts her when he finds that she had been almost a prostitute at home.

Captain's pride is a potted palm he won for efficient cargo-loading. But the crew hates it as a symbol of tyranny, for to win it the Captain (William Harrigan) made their lives hell.

While cleaning a spyglass, one crewman finds he can see ashore into a hospital window. He calls his buddies (right) and they feast on the sight of pretty nurses taking showers.

A nurse from the hospital hears the crew betting she is the one with a mole on her backside. She discovers the showers are visible from the ship, orders curtains put up, and the crew mourns its little paradise lost.

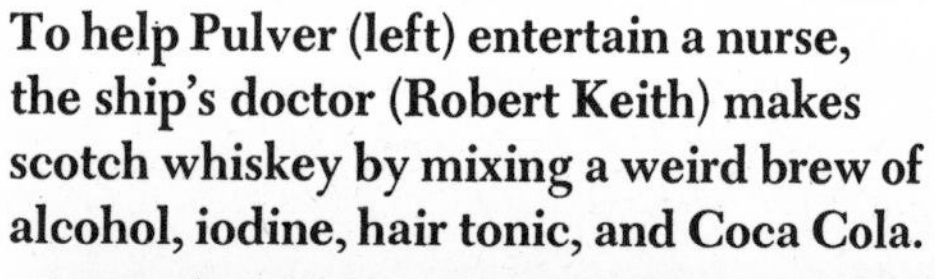
To help Pulver (left) entertain a nurse, the ship's doctor (Robert Keith) makes scotch whiskey by mixing a weird brew of alcohol, iodine, hair tonic, and Coca Cola.

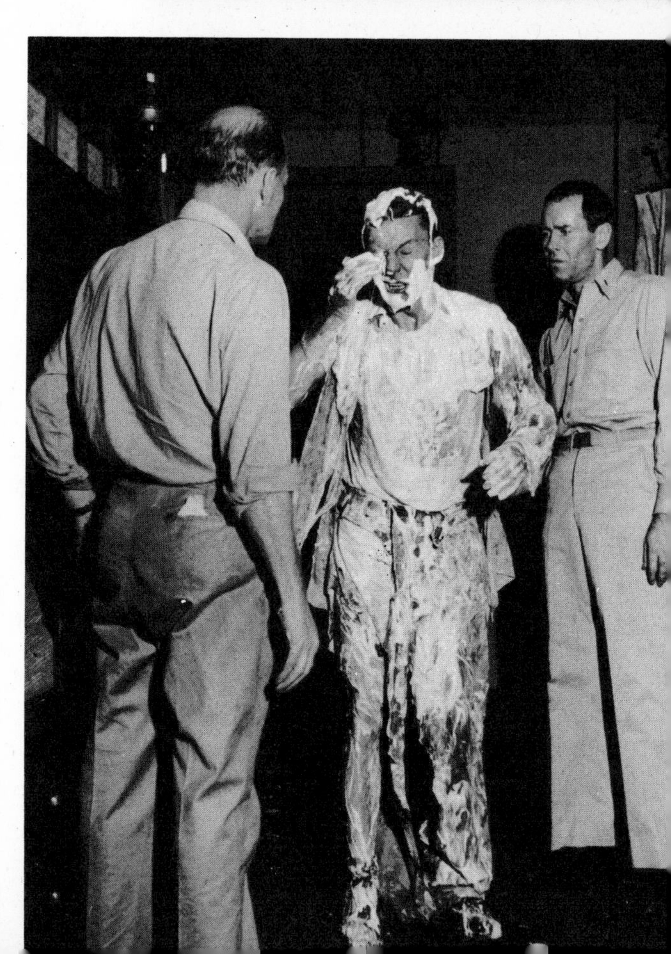

Mister Roberts

Henry Fonda plays the heroic Mr. Roberts who defends his crew against the captain's tyranny and continuously dreams of getting himself transferred to a combat ship.

The best straight drama to come out of World War II was *Mister Roberts,* a rough-talking but poignant dramatization by Joshua Logan and Thomas Heggen of Heggen's story about the boredom of 167 men on a Pacific cargo ship "on its regular run from Tedium to Apathy." Faultlessly directed by Logan, the show opened in 1948 for a three-year Broadway run and had three road companies simultaneously playing to packed houses throughout the U.S. In the title role as a lieutenant j.g. who is idolized by the crew and tyrannized by a stupid captain, movie star Henry Fonda turned in a magnificently quiet and humorous performance.

A tribute to Roberts is paid by Pulver when he tosses the Captain's new palm overboard. He has just learned that Roberts, finally getting into combat, has been killed off Okinawa.

Disaster overtakes Ensign Pulver (David Wayne) when on V.E. day he experiments with some homemade firecrackers in the ship's laundry and almost drowns himself in an explosion of suds.

Willy Loman (Lee J. Cobb) idolizes his football-playing sons, Hap and Biff (Cameron Mitchell, Arthur Kennedy), and teaches them to believe in easy fame.

Death of a Salesman

Willy's devoted wife (Mildred Dunnock) upbraids her sons for neglecting their father. "Attention must be paid," she says. "He must not be allowed to fall into his grave like an old dog."

Despair engulfs Willy (below) whenever he remembers the awful moment when Biff caught him in a Boston hotel with a woman and forever after doubted his father's honesty.

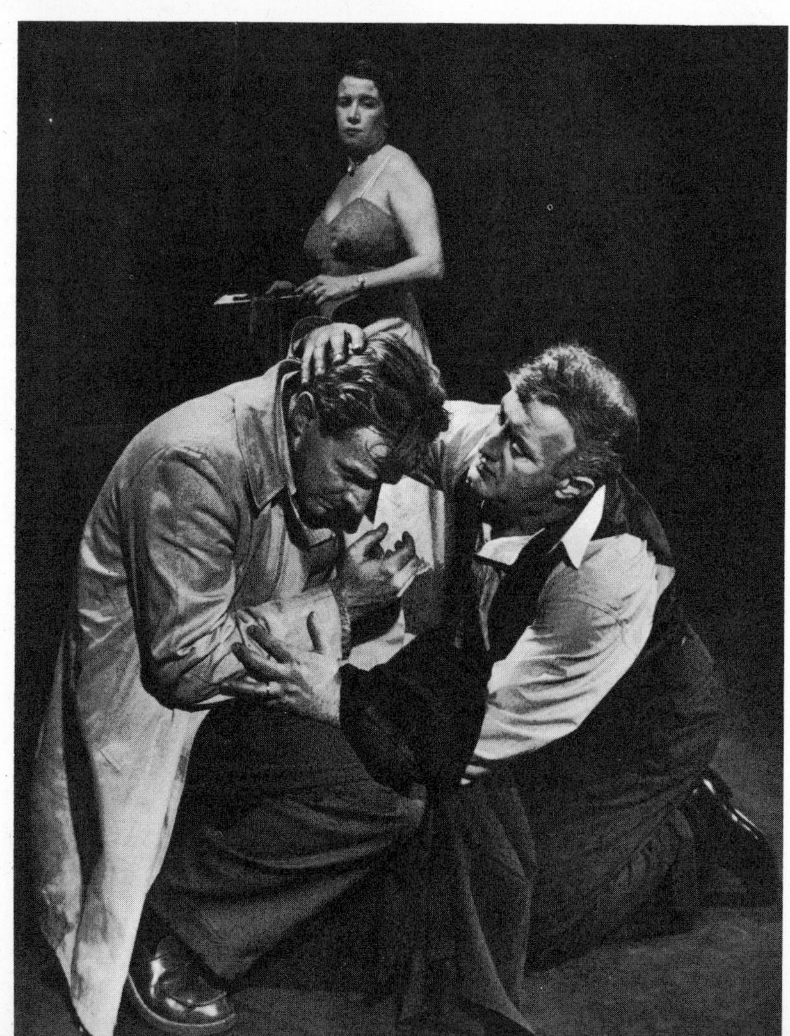

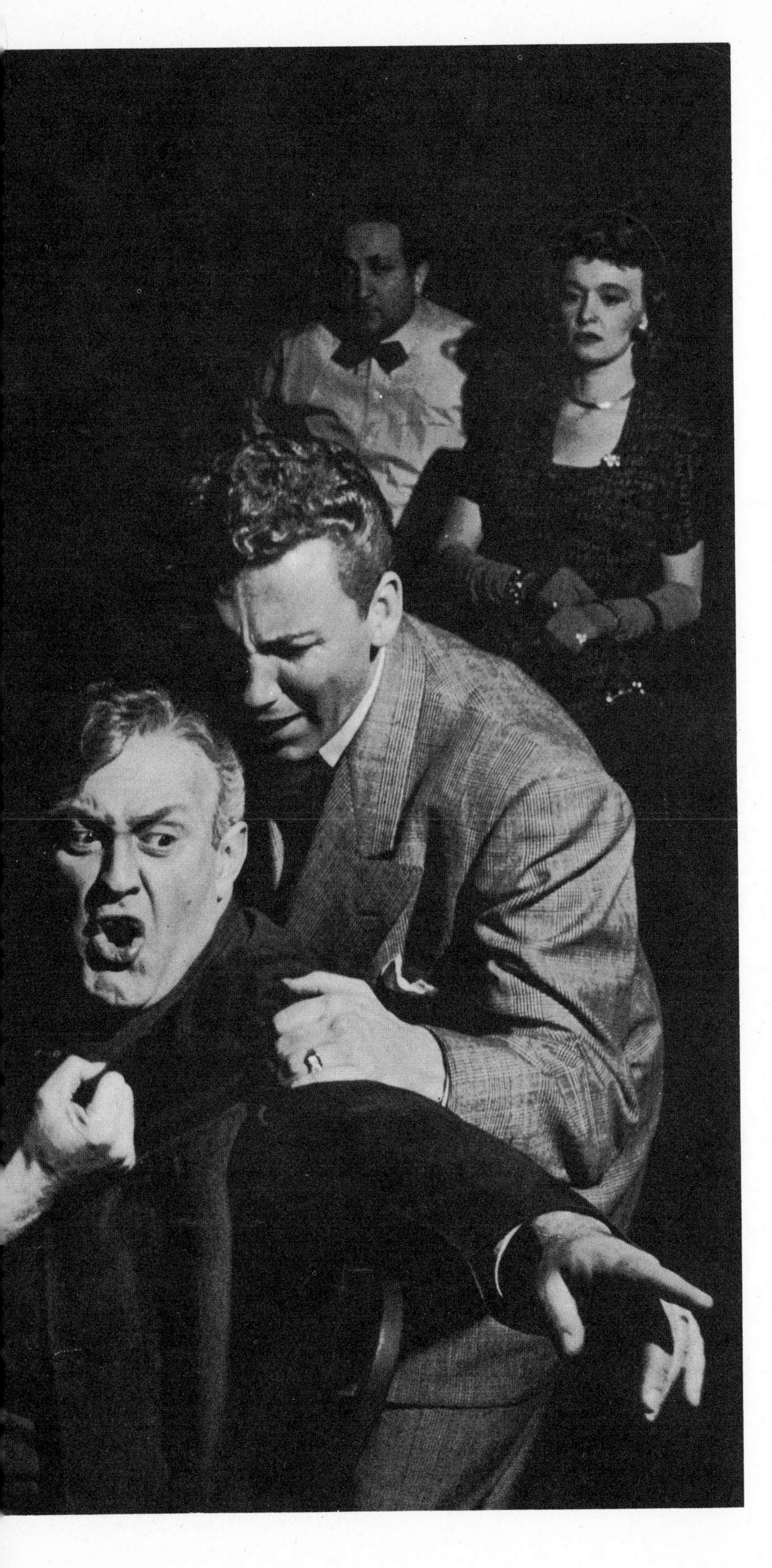

Losing his mind from worrying over his business failure, Willy babbles at imaginary characters in a restaurant. His sons try to quiet him while two floozies the boys have picked up look on in cold puzzlement.

Arthur Miller's 1949 hit is one of the outstanding tragedies ever written by an American. Its tragic hero is Willy Loman, a big-hearted, big-talking Brooklyn salesman who imbues his two beloved sons with his callow credo: "Personality always wins the day . . . be liked and you'll never want." The play derives much of its emotional power from Miller's warm understanding of the relationship between a father and his sons. But, inevitably, both father and sons suffocate on their own hot air and Willy goes miserably to his death, a good man with "the wrong dream."

At Willy's funeral, after his suicide, his wife kneels devoutly while his friend pays a tribute to the salesman: "He's a man out there in the blue, ridin' on a smile and a shoeshine . . . A salesman has got to dream, boys; it comes with the territory."

The Member of the Wedding

Feeling unloved, Frankie forgets her sorrow by being a tomboy. Roughly she digs a splinter from her foot (top), shadow-boxes, and then gives way to little-girl longings.

Frankie and her nextdoor playmate, John Henry (Brandon de Wilde) learn wisdom from Big Berenice (Ethel Waters).

Frankie beams at her brother and fiancee whose wedding for her is a supreme event. Frankie plans to go on honeymoon, share their bliss forever.

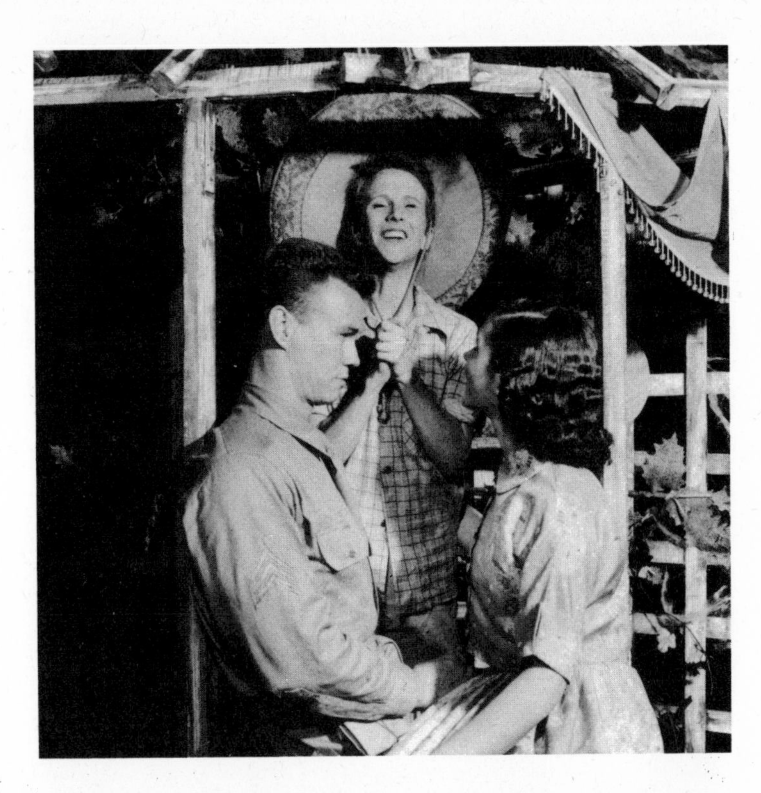

Carson McCullers' hit, which opened on Broadway in 1950, proved that the modern U.S. stage was not wholly committed to the conventional well-made-play. Here was hardly a play at all, but a poetic character sketch of a 12-year-old tomboy and her fierce desire to feel needed and loved. Acted beautifully by Ethel Waters and Julie Harris, and directed by Harold Clurman, Miss McCullers' success in the theatre was a credit to everyone.

Frankie shows off an absurd dress she bought for the wedding. Though in the end she is rejected by the honeymooners, she outgrows her tomboyhood, heads rightly towards maturity.

I Am a Camera

John Van Druten, most productive of current dramatists, based his most interesting play on a group of short stories by Christopher Isherwood. Its heroine is Sally, a silly, slangy, amoral, completely charming English girl who runs away from her family to a Bohemian life in pre-Hitler Berlin, a life compounded of long binges and briefly broken hearts. Sally epitomizes many ills of her day. So, too, does her all-seeing but passive friend, Christopher, who says of himself, "I am a camera."

Sally starts on another forlorn chase after romance, leaving behind a forlorn Christopher who is unable to say how much he has come to love her.

Lola dances a rumba for her husband, Doc (Sidney Blackmer), who wants only to read his paper.

Rage begins to boil over in Doc when, after an all-night binge, he is questioned by Lola.

Come Back, Little Sheba

With this 1950 play a new dramatist, William Inge, stepped into the spotlight. As unforgettable as any recent stage portrait was Lola De Laney, acted superbly by Shirley Booth, who waddled around her sloppy house in bedroom slippers, munched chocolates, devoured radio soap operas, fatuously mourned her lost puppy, Sheba, and drove her husband to drink. What gave the play importance and poignance was Lola's innate decency and capacity to suffer.

Attacking Lola with a hatchet, Doc in a drunken frenzy threatens to "hack off all that fat."

Watching a girl boarder kissing a college athlete reminds Doc, by contrast, of his own drab married life.

Bleary with drunkenness, Doc still has enough spirit to struggle on toward a better life with Lola.

After escaping from an asylum Virginia (Margo) drifts into the World Wide steam laundry (on steps, left). She is befriended and taken home by a worker named John, and, to conceal her past, gives her name as Hariett Hope.

The World We Make

Like a crack reporter getting to the core of a news event, Sidney Kingsley has written a series of vivid documentary-like dramas. In 1939 *The World We Make,* based on a Millen Brand novel, was a case history of a genteel girl who escapes from a mental hospital and, by wandering into a crude but forthright world of work and love, regains health.

In the tenement where John lives, Hariett starts a new life. She takes pride in tidying up his home, learns from kindly neighbors how to help herself and help others.

In her first night at John's home, Hariett cowers in bed while he quiets her by reading Dickens. She finds he needs her as much as she needs him, and eventually they marry.

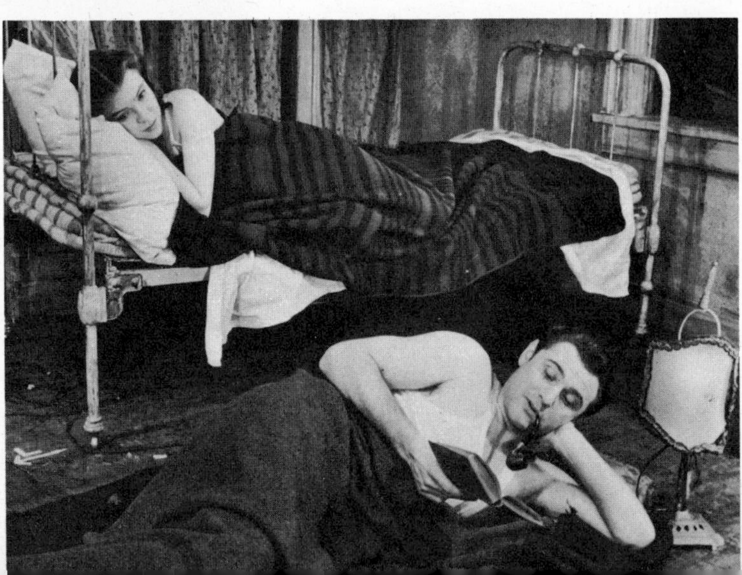

Darkness at Noon

Another Kingsley play, taken from Arthur Koestler's study of the scandalous 1937 Moscow trials, was *Darkness at Noon,* which was produced in 1951. The stage action focuses on the last six weeks in the life of an imprisoned commissar and Red general, Rubashov, showing how he is induced to falsely confess his guilt. Rubashov was excellently acted by Claude Rains.

"Is it day or night outside? What day? Month? Who are you?" These messages are being tapped out in code from cell to cell in this Moscow prison scene which opened the play. The new prisoner, Rubashov (below left) goes to his doom, a victim of his own false philosophy.

Professor Turner (Eliott Nugent) gets hilariously drunk with one of his students and boasts that he feels the same male ferocity as the bull elephant, the tiger, sea hawks and brave little land crabs.

Asserting his manhood, the professor recaptures his wife from a more athletic wolf, who ducks out the door and returns to his own wife.

The Male Animal

As a stage hero the modern American male is not a figure of high deeds or firm purpose. There is a hint of ineffectiveness about him, as if he were more a dupe than a doer. One of the most engaging heroes, however, was the droll young professor in The Male Animal by James Thurber and Elliott Nugent (a hit in 1940 and revived successfully in 1952). This hero, mild and bumbling at first, finally pulled himself together, stood up for the rights of liberalism in a U. S. university and won his wife away from a brawnier ex-football idol.

This hero (Ralph Meeker) finds approval in the eyes of a Kansas housewife when he comes around looking for odd jobs and ends up toting a trash can.

Bewildered by an uncertain world, the footloose hero still wins the prettiest girl in town (Janice Rule) and together they are fortified by their love.

Another male animal—more predatory than the Thurber-Nugent specimen (opposite page)—was hero of 1953's Pulitzer Prize winner, *Picnic,* by William Inge. Cocky and vigorous, he strode into the backyard lives of some middle-class Kansans, and as a hero-symbol brought them a measure of joy and fulfillment. Despite his power to give and win love, he himself was insecure and rootless, and faced a hazardous future.

Picnic

The frisky citizens of Catfish Row conduct a crap game under the wicked eye of a flashy gambler named Sportin' Life (Cab Calloway).

Porgy and Bess

About the closest thing to an American stage classic is the opera, *Porgy and Bess,* based on a play by Dorothy and DuBose Heyward. With music by George Gershwin and lyrics by his gifted brother, Ira, and DuBose Heyward, it tells the story of a crippled Negro, Porgy, and his love for the prettiest girl in Catfish Row. Musically, *Porgy and Bess* stems more from Broadway than South Carolina, but, though it is impure Negro opera, it is pure and rousing theatre.

The beautiful Bess (Leontyne Price) tries to free herself from the tentacles of Sportin' Life, who sells her dope.

A brutal Negro, Crown, who terrorizes Catfish Row, boasts that he has stolen Bess once from Porgy, and is going to steal her again.

After Porgy has killed Crown, and Bess has been lured off to New York by Sportin' Life, Porgy kneels on his little goat cart, and valiantly starts North to find her.

Taking to drink to relieve her fears, the Medium sees scary visions, sings a long, wild aria, falls into a drunken stupor, wakes to murder the mute.

In 1947, a full-fledged musical play, *The Medium*, startled Broadway with its amalgam of beautiful music and weird melodrama. The story traced the fate of a fake spiritualist who finally becomes a victim of her own deceptions and begins to feel a ghostly hand at her throat. Written, composed, and directed by 35-year-old Gian-Carlo Menotti, *The Medium* was turned into an equally gripping movie and made critics wonder whether the U.S. cannot actually create first-class opera.

In her gloomy Victorian parlor, Medium (Marie Powers) holds a séance while her young daughter impersonates the ghost of a client's dead child, singing an eerie chant: "Mother, mother, are you there . . . ?"

In a wild fury born of her terror, the Medium ends the séance, orders her startled clients to leave after she feels the grip of a cold hand at her throat. Cowering on the floor are her mute assistant and her daughter.

The Medium

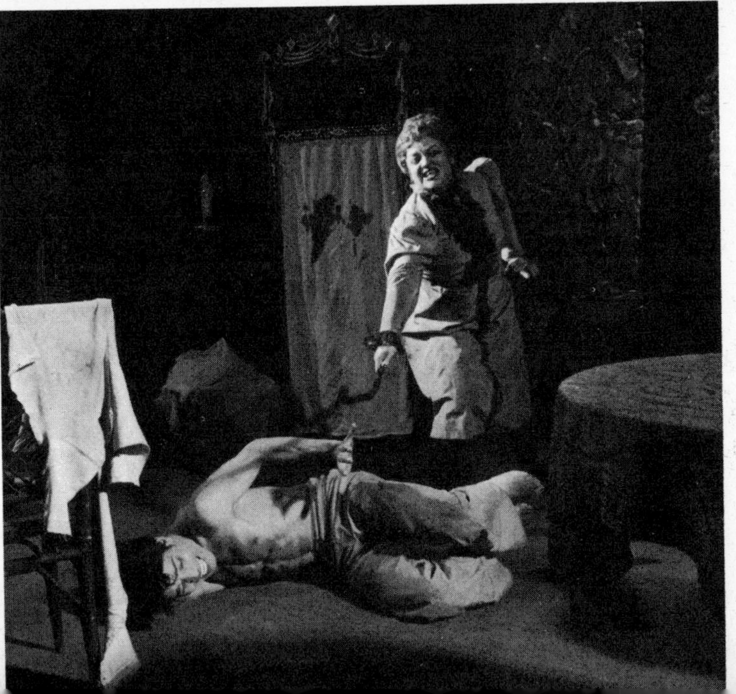

The tragedy of the opera is rooted in the Medium's belief that the mute, who operates mechanical controls for séances, is "the ghost" of her mounting hallucinations. Here, she whips him because he won't confess.

While secret police hunt her husband, Magda Sorel (Patricia Neway, center) and her mother-in-law refuse to tell them he is hiding in the loft above.

During agonizing waits in consul's office, a magician relieves tension by hypnotizing Magda and others into thinking they're at a ball.

The Consul

Three years after his surprise hit, *The Medium,* Gian-Carlo Menotti did it again with another music drama, *The Consul.* It was the grim saga of a wife's frantic attempts to get a visa to join her husband, hounded out of his country by fascist secret police "somewhere in Europe." She is tragically trapped by consular red tape and human indifference.

In a fury after endless waiting, Magda rips up senseless papers she had to sign.

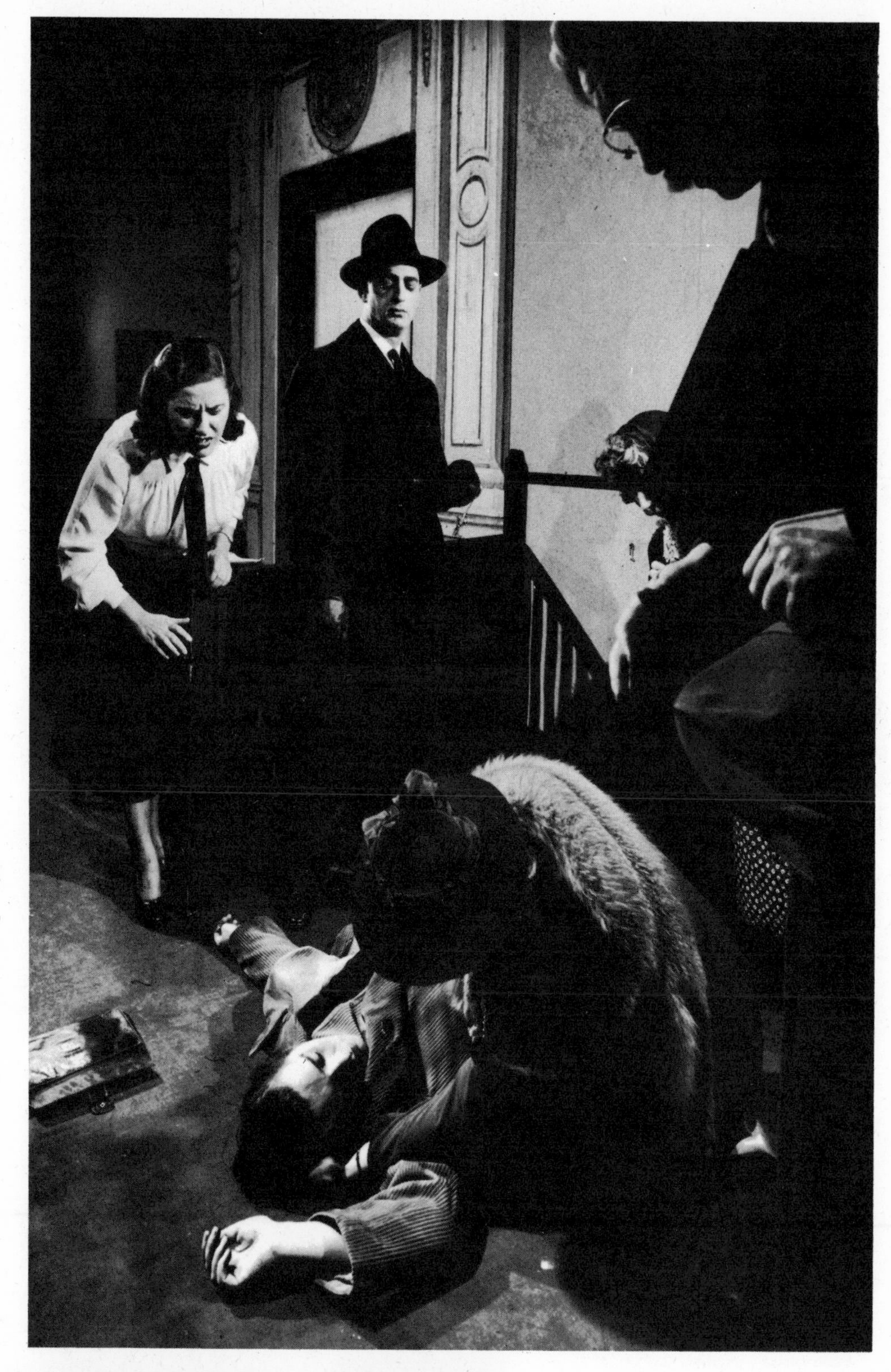

Told she can see the consul at last, Magda sees his door open for her arch-foe, the secret police chief. Knowing she is doomed, she swoons.

In despair, Magda turn on the gas in her flat, has wild hopeless dreams, dies.

Mother Day was first acted by Dorothy Stickney, surrounded here by her five red-headed problems. The four sons were (left to right): Whitney (Raymond Roe), Clarence, Jr. (John Drew Devereaux), John (Richard Simon), Harlan (Larry Robinson). The benign tyrant she married was Howard Lindsay.

Life with Father

Like an animated family album, *Life with Father* opened its lively pages in New York in 1939 and ran for 3224 performances, an all-time record for any show on Broadway. The play, written by Howard Lindsay and Russel Crouse, was based on a series of sketches by Clarence Day, Jr., which described his own New York childhood under the choleric but kindly eye of father.

Clowns and Carnivals

Since most modern drama has become boxed inside the three walls of stage realism, the only theatre which consistently makes room for imagination, fantasy, poetry (of sorts), and cock-eyed flights of wit and slapstick is the theatre of musical shows and comedians. Anything goes in this carnival world; anything, that is, which has its own truth and vitality. America, particularly in the past quarter century, has erupted with comedians and musical shows, as if something untrammeled in the national psyche refused to knuckle under to the legitimate theatre's meek and orderly way of making make-believe too believable.

Compared to the clowns and comedians of other countries, the funnymen of the U.S.A. tend to be less critical or satirical and more plain nonsensical. The Jimmy Durantes, Ed Wynns, Phil Silverses, and Danny Kayes are almost all pure zany. Europeans are often surprised that American comedians rely so little on off-color innuendo. Our stage humor is predominantly clean—clean but crazy. European comics, with their outbursts of bawdiness, express revolt against the proprieties; American comics, on the other hand, are generally in revolt against order. They are anarchists whose value to an over-mechanized, over-orderly nation is incalculable.

For its progress in the field of musical comedy the U.S. theatre of late has done a good bit of preening. Undeniably there has been a steady improvement in the quality of show music, beginning with Victor Herbert and Jerome Kern, and continuing with Gershwin, Rodgers, Berlin, Porter, Youmans, Schwartz, Loesser, and Arlen. Undeniably, too, there is more and more visual good taste. The glittering *Follies* extravaganzas, which still persist in a few Paris and London showhouses, were fun to gaze upon uncritically, but their lost tinsel cannot seriously be deplored. Today many of the theatre's most imaginative stage settings find their way into Broadway musicals designed by Meilziner, Ayres, Dubois, and Smith; and in the costume department such designers as Ballard and Sharaff contribute real elegance and excitement. Modern ballet has become a standard ingredient of Broadway shows, and sometimes gets out of hand. But even the die-hard admirers of an old-fashioned buck-and-wing, or of the traditional line of simultaneously kicking cuties, admit that such choreographers as Robbins, Kidd, and Tamiris have added new beauty and new meaning to dozens of musicals, and kept in the old sex, too.

Probably the most important pioneers in the song and dance field were Composer Richard Rodgers and Lyricist Lorenz Hart, who gradually through their charming and witty songs raised the level of taste. After Hart's death, Rodgers continued to dominate Broadway with his new collaborator, Oscar Hammerstein II. Their half-dozen shows, uneven as they are, have done more than anything else to broaden and elevate the popular musical theatre. The influence of Cole Porter, too, is unique. By blending a number of musical styles—Latin American, Jewish, Negro, French—he has created an individual style, which, combined with his own expert lyrics, has given us songs that in years to come may evoke most precisely the metropolitan mood of the mid-twentieth century.

American musical comedy could be better. It needs more bite as well as beauty, more fun as well as fantasy. It needs a bigger dash of Aristophanes, of Plautus, of Congreve. But it can stand up under criticism because its potentialities are so great.

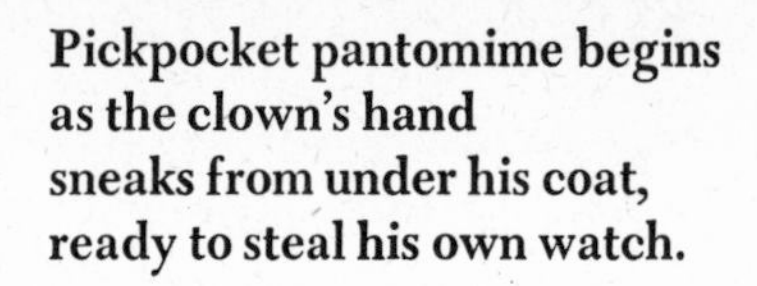

Pickpocket pantomime begins as the clown's hand sneaks from under his coat, ready to steal his own watch.

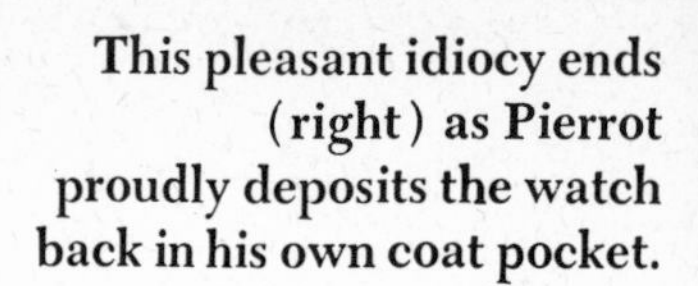

This pleasant idiocy ends (right) as Pierrot proudly deposits the watch back in his own coat pocket.

With consternation Pierrot discovers that his watch is missing, has no idea who could have taken it.

With astonishment and delight Pierrot finds that the missing watch is in his own right hand.

Jean Louis Barrault

The ancient art of pantomime, which blossomed in the impromptu buffoonery (*commedia dell' arte*) of strolling Italian street players and has been carried on by circus clowns and burlesque comedians, is revived in its early form by Jean Louis Barrault. This distinguished French actor, who brought his own dramatic repertory company from Paris to New York in 1952, is a perfect prototype of Pierrot. In a short sketch, shown here, Barrault recreates the traditional sad-faced clown, confusing himself by stealing his own watch.

Outside his marvelous Mississippi show boat, Captain Andy introduces his star performer, Julie.

Show Boat

Bloodcurdling melodrama is enacted on the show-boat stage where Magnolia is attacked by the villain (Buddy Ebsen).

At their wedding Magnolia and Ravenal roll off in a rose-covered carriage, destined for a rocky future.

Magnolia (Jan Clayton), Andy's daughter, has a romantic but sad marriage with Ravenal.

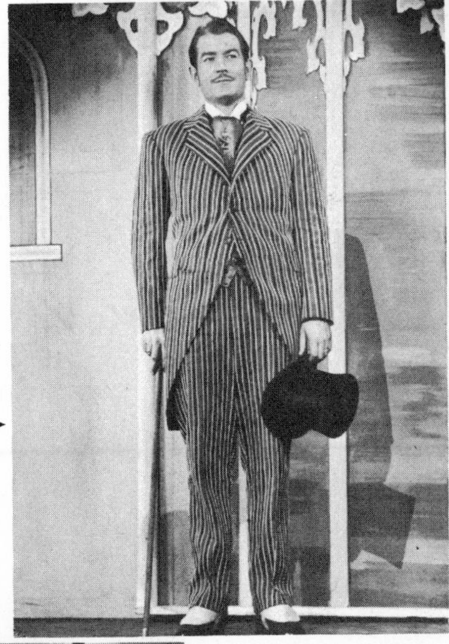

Parthy Ann (Ethel Owen) is Captain Andy's gingery wife who keeps him comically henpecked.

In the field of popular operetta nothing quite compares with *Show Boat*, adapted from Edna Ferber's novel by Oscar Hammerstein II and composer Jerome Kern. A fine stagy vitality springs from its characters, which seem to have real passions and big troubles. Then, of course, there are Kern's songs, for simple eloquence so hard to beat and even harder to forget. These pictures are from the 1946 revival.

"He's just my Bill," sings warm-hearted Julie (Carol Bruce), whose dash of Negro blood brings her grief.

Ravenal (Charles Fredericks) is the dashing gambler who cannot provide for his wife.

Joe (Kenneth Spencer) works on the showboat and sings the stirring "Ol' Man River."

Pal Joey

Spoofing idiotic night club spectacles, this girl (left) in the 1952 *Pal Joey*, represents "Violets."
Below she turns around to reveal her violets modishly placed.

Pal Joey, based on short stories by John O'Hara and with songs by Richard Rodgers and Lorenz Hart, proved that an American musical comedy could sustain a biting and adult point of view. Its hero, Joey, is a no-good Chicago nightclub hoofer, who has a plushy time as a rich matron's plaything, and then does an off-to-Buffalo to obscurity.

Harold Lang as the 1952 Joey did a wonderful job of dancing, helped make the show a greater popular hit than it was in 1942.

In the original production, Gene Kelly was the hoofer who tried to snare a pretty girl by tossing her a line about his aristocratic family.

Gene Kelly (opposite page) danced the title role brilliantly, created the precisely right blend of cad and Casanova. After Joey, he took his talents to Hollywood.

In his dreams of glory, Joey imagines himself dancing in a swank club plucking cigarettes from the headdress of a beautiful show girl.

Joey finds glory only as a rich matron's gigolo, here singing "In Our Little Den of Iniquity." The matron was acted by Vivienne Segal, who again in 1952 did the same part superbly.

An aquatic love story begins when a tipsy lady at a high-class garden party jumps in the pool and dallies with a statue who, naturally, comes to life.

Showing off, the statue leads her to his underwater court peopled by harp-playing nymphs and fishermen. The lady likes it and decides to join her friend by becoming a statue herself.

A "Folies" star, Yvonne Menard steps onto a runway in front of orchestra conductor to act as mistress of ceremonies, chat with audience, and just have fun.

This world-famous Paris revue is a remote cousin to the elaborate masques and spectacles which used to enliven European courts. The *Folies* lures thousands of tourists every year, offers them an agreeable dash of nudity and a knockout dose of fantastic razzle-dazzle (see above) which seems to have been designed to delight visiting Argentine cattle kings.

Yvonne appears again in a characteristic "Folies" number, "New Orleans," which is innocent of meaning.

Folies Bergère

Jimmy Durante

From out of Hollywood comes this example of the lengths to which certain creatures will go to get their pictures published. This squirrel is homely, small, and its tail is not particularly bushy. Untidily dressed, it has an unsightly gap between jacket and belt; its face is unshaven and rodentlike. Nonetheless it is posed arrogantly at the piano exactly as though it were capable of playing something. The truth is that the squirrel has absolutely no talent and cannot even carry a tune. . . . The man partially visible in the background is a bit actor who is appearing with the squirrel in a movie called *The Great Rupert*.

He invents a wrist-sponge to keep asparagus from dripping up his sleeve.

A thimble gimmick permits him to dunk bread in gravy without soiling his fingers.

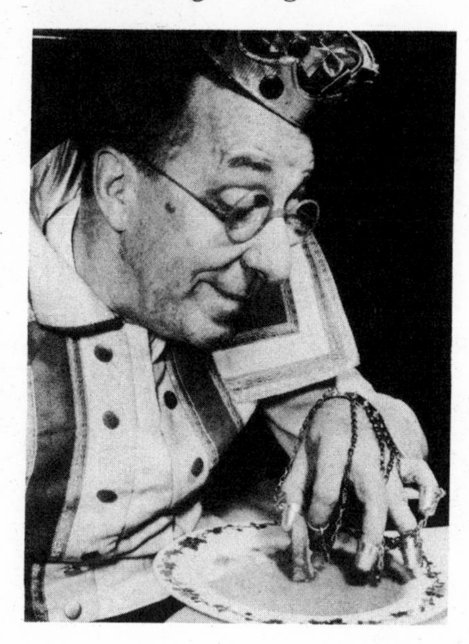

Ear of corn turns on a typewriter roller, rings when he comes to end of cob.

Ed Wynn

One of the greatest American stage clowns is Ed Wynn. He combines all kinds of sight-gags —visual devices to make people laugh—with a wild, fairy-tale personality composed of lisping innocence, giggling delight, and a mad absorption in his own mad world.

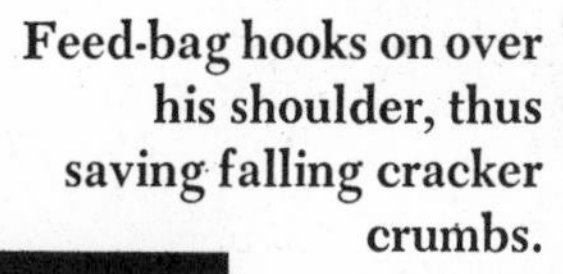

Feed-bag hooks on over his shoulder, thus saving falling cracker crumbs.

Shade pulls down over face to protect him from squirting grapefruit juice.

Combination fork and nose guard enables him to eat smelly cheese in comfort.

Oklahoma!

"People Will Say We're in Love" is sung by Curly and Laurie (Alfred Drake, Joan Roberts) as they begin to feel connubially inclined.

In a dream interlude Laurie and Curly are united in a cowboy wedding, enacted by ballet dancers.

Here is a landmark in U.S. theatre history. It was the first teamwork of author Oscar Hammerstein II and composer Richard Rodgers, set a new style for less flashy musicals, and became one of the most loved of all Broadway shows. Its excellent ballet, directed by Agnes De Mille, started an epidemic of Broadway ballets, both good and terrible. Its story, based on a Lynn Riggs play, concerned itself simply with what happened when Cowboy Curly invited Laurie to an Oklahoma box supper.

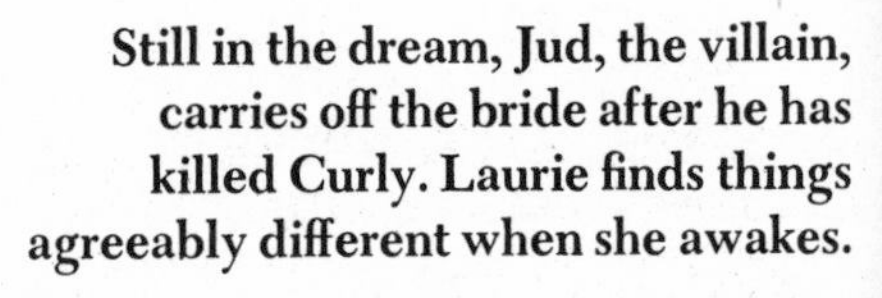

Still in the dream, Jud, the villain, carries off the bride after he has killed Curly. Laurie finds things agreeably different when she awakes.

"I Cain't Say No," the lament of a girl who is susceptible to men, is sung by Celeste Holm as Ado Annie.

"The Surrey With the Fringe on Top" is sung by Curly to Laurie, and turns up in reality at the end to take the newlyweds on a honeymoon.

Zanies

The great zanies are created and pressed into shape by society itself, by its laughter and applause, and by the silent sympathy and understanding that surround them. They are fantastic offspring of the collective mind, and, standing with the saints and heroes, they belong with the world's treasures.

A hedonist triumphant, Groucho Marx is master of his fate, master of the world, master of delicious women.

The monumental W. C. Fields burped at the universe, well aware that all life is a preposterous fraud.

Bert Lahr, passion's plaything, tickles the ankle of Betty Grable and yelps at the pain and wonder of it.

Jimmy Savo, in his goblin powers, gently bids the river stay away from his door.

Robert Benchley, doing his Treasurer's Report, laid bare the poor, befuddled mind of man.

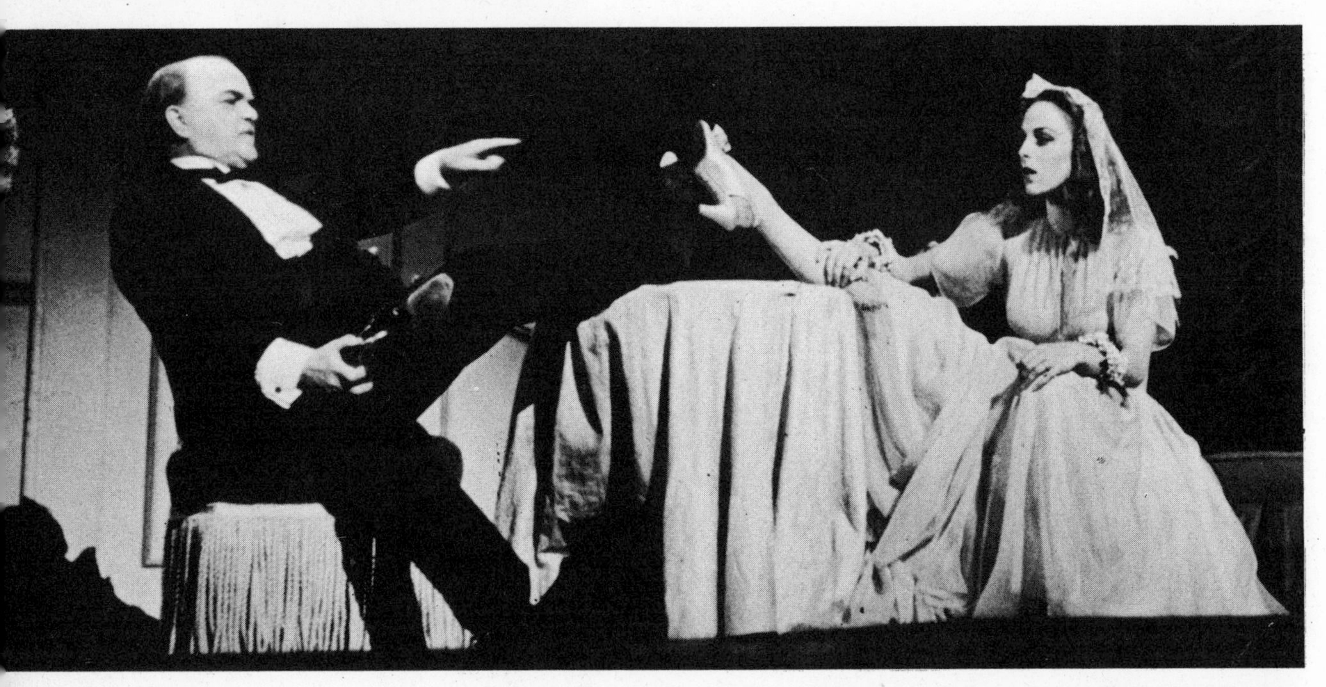

Victor Moore, displaying a hole in his sock to Vera Zorina, shows how man is undone by small miseries.

N'S CAROUSEL

To get money to care for their expected baby, Billy goes off to take part in a hold-up. His wife, suspecting he is up to no good, tries to hold him back.

Carousel

Ferenc Molnar's famous play *Liliom* was adapted by Oscar Hammerstein II and Richard Rodgers into one of the best musical shows ever produced in America (1945). Its fantastic bittersweet plot, transplanted from Hungary to New England, still retains its rascally hero who falls in love, behaves badly, dies, tries to enter heaven, and then returns to earth for awhile to learn the deepest meaning of love.

At left Billy Bigelow (John Raitt) sparks Julie (Jan Clayton) on a carousel horse, while a minor ruckus goes on at the side.

In heaven the Starkeeper tells Billy he cannot enter the premises until he goes back to earth and does one good deed.

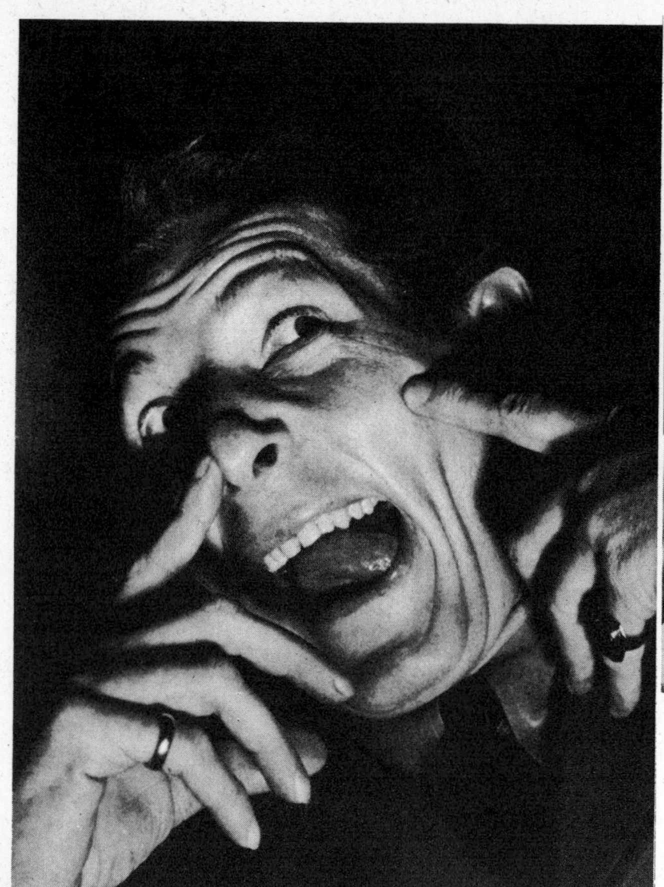

Let's Face It

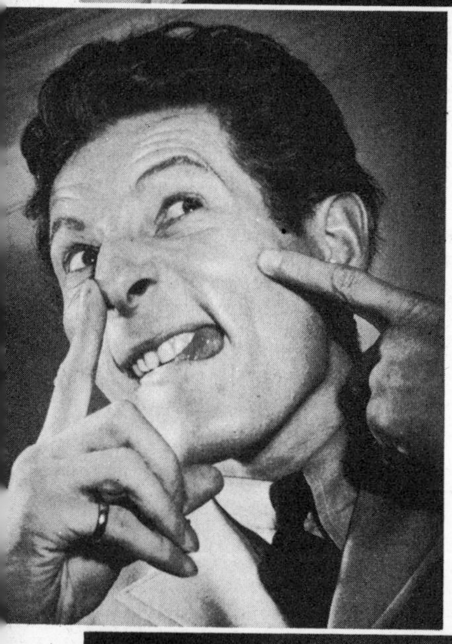

Three rookies on a visit get an unexpected glimpse of home life.

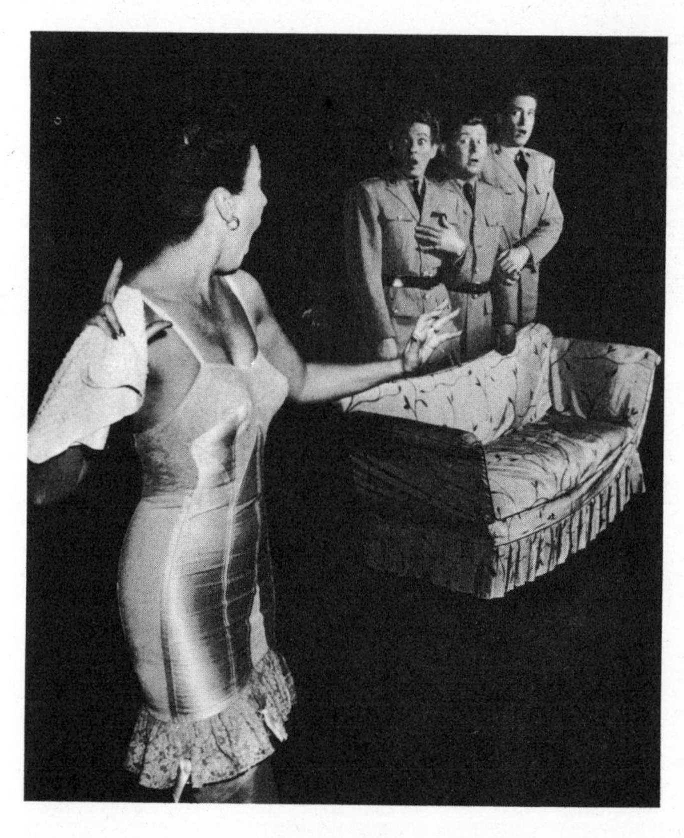

This 1941 girl show had no significance whatsoever except that, dealing with the vicissitudes of young draftees, it reflected America's invincibly optimistic attitude towards war. In it a budding performer named Danny Kaye (left) did a git-gat-gittle song that established him as a top comedian.

Against a red, white, and blue backdrop these young ladies testify to the supremacy of American legs.

Sono Osato poses in front of a huge blowup of a placard which announces her election as "Miss Turnstiles," queen of New York subways.

On the subway the three sailors, Gabey, Chip and Ozzie, see the placard of Miss Turnstiles. When Gabey raves about it, they set out to find her.

Searching for Miss Turnstiles, Sailor Chip meets a female cab driver (Nancy Walker), who yanks him into her cab while singing Come Up to My Place.

Still on the search, Sailor Ozzie visits the Museum of Natural History and has a fling with a lady anthropologist, who regards him merely as a specimen.

On the Town

At Coney, Gabey see his dream girl, who is momentarily upset that he has found out about her. But they steal a few hours of joy before his leave is up and all three gobs depart.

On the Town, a Broadway hit at the start of World War II, told of three Navy Sinbads taking shore leave on the bizarre isle of Manhattan. Going deeper than most musicals, this one managed to be both comic and poignant, suggested the now-or-never feeling of young people trying to cram all they can of love and pleasure into a few short hours. The show had music by Leonard Bernstein, dances by Jerome Robbins, and book and lyrics by a new team, Betty Comden and Adolph Green. All under 28, they went on to shine in their respective fields.

Miss Turnstiles is tracked down by Gabey in Carnegie Hall where she studies singing with a tipsy teacher. To earn a living, Miss T. is a kootch dancer at Coney Island.

Disappointed in love, Ethel Merman as Annie Oakley, the backwoods sharp-shooter, bemoans her fate in "You Can't Get a Man With a Gun." But she does get a job in Buffalo Bill's show assisting her hero, Frank Butler.

Annie's greatest stunt is shooting out eight candles on a revolving ring while riding a motorcycle. This display of female skill injures the male pride of sharp-shooting Frank Butler, who fears Annie will outshine him.

Annie's joy at having just learned how to read turns to sorrow when the letter turns out to be a farewell note from Frank, who has stalked off in a snit to join Pawnee Bill's rival show. Her sympathetic friend is Sitting Bull.

Annie Get Your Gun

In a final tableau, styled after an old Wild West poster, Buffalo Bill and Pawnee Bill have merged professionally, while Annie and Frank have merged romantically.

A high order of popular Broadway showmanship in 1946 produced *Annie Get Your Gun,* a musical extravaganza based on an actual romance between a famed American markswoman, Annie Oakley, and another sharp-shooter, Frank Butler. To embellish the book by Dorothy and Herbert Fields, Irving Berlin wrote words and music for 15 songs, which were as bright as anything he ever produced in 40 years of making Americans whistle and dance. Annie was played by Ethel Merman, who was wonderful.

Gorilla meets girl in one of the memorable moments of the modern theatre. It happened in the Mack Sennett ballet, directed by Jerome Robbins, in *High Button Shoes* (1947), which spoofed the old-time two-reel movie comedies.

High Button Shoes

Prof. Lamberti

A very great man was the late Professor Lamberti, seen in Michael Todd's revue, *Star and Garter* (1942). His famous act consisted of playing wildly on the xylophone while a beautiful girl, unseen by him, wanders on and does a strip tease. As the audience applauds more and more, the good professor assumes the appreciation is all for him. Dizzy with success, he knocks himself out trying to play louder and faster—which indicates something about the vanity of men and the wisdom of women.

As Nellie the Navy nurse,
Mary Martin finds love
in the arms of Ezio Pinza,
singing *Some Enchanted Evening*

South Pacific

Urged on by her mother,
a shy native lass finds love
with a Marine, singing *Happy Talk*

In the camp show
Mary Martin as a gob ogles
Myron McCormick as an island siren.

With the children of the French planter whom she hopes to wed, Mary tensely scans the sky for the plane she prays will bring him back from a perilous mission.

To celebrate her new romance Mary cavorts among her nurse friends and sings *I'm in Love with a Wonderful Guy.*

South Pacific opened on Broadway in 1949, won a Pulitzer prize as the year's best play, and will probably go down as the most successful musical show in stage history. It is the work of Composer Richard Rodgers and Writers Oscar Hammerstein II and Joshua Logan. Its homespun heroine is Nellie Forbush, a Navy nurse from Arkansas serving on a Pacific isle. Nellie falls in love with the least likely suitor she can imagine, a middle-aged French planter who is a widower with two children. The biggest hit to emerge from World War II, *South Pacific* makes a plea for racial tolerance and flaunts its idealism frankly in contrast to the heedless and raucous hit of World War I, *What Price Glory?*

In her low slung sailor pants
Mary Martin cuts loose with some high kicks

Kiss Me Kate

Lisa Kirk sang a playfully cynical little ballad with the refrain, "I'm always true to you, darlin', in my fashion."

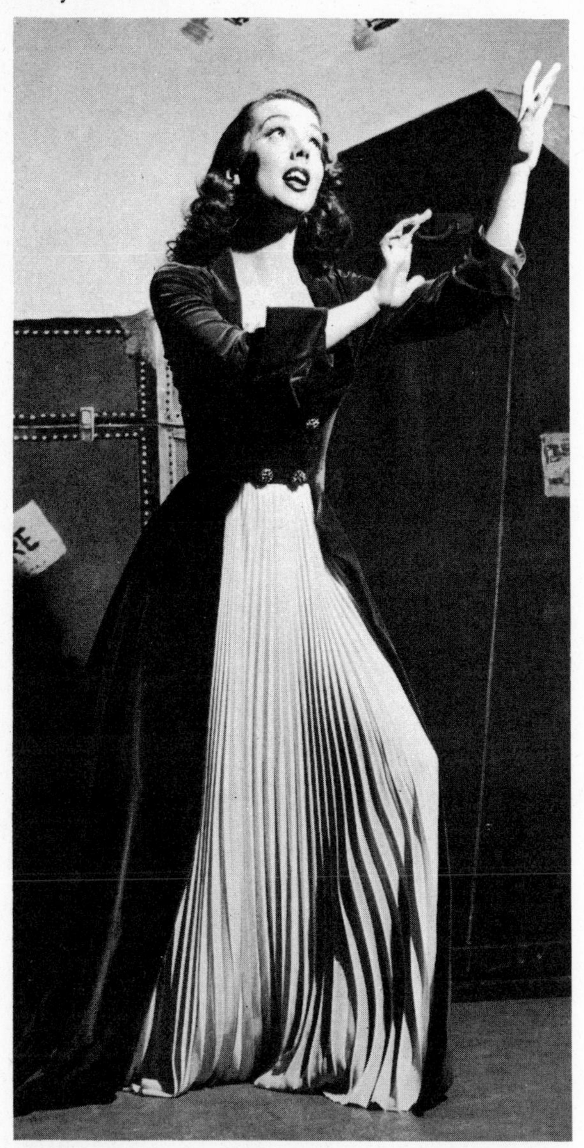

Alfred Drake and Patricia Morison played the shrew and her husband with manifest enjoyment.

The free-wheeling gusto and extravagance of American musical comedy was displayed fully and stridently in the 1948 hit, *Kiss Me Kate*. A double-decker affair, it sandwiched the backstage bickering of an actor and his ex-wife with their on-stage scrapping as newlyweds in Shakespeare's *Taming of the Shrew*. It had gorgeous costumes, snappy dancing, sophisticated clowning, but especially the raciest of all words-and-music jobs by Cole Porter.

A pair of dapper gangsters extolled culture in a patter song called "Brush up your Shakespeare."

Harold Lang went high-flying to the percussive beat of the song, "It's Too Darn Hot."

Guys and Dolls

Epic crap game is held in spacious sewer where Masterson (Robert Alda), after being converted by his mission sweetheart, rolls dice on a bet to make his sinner cronies come to her mission.

Show begins with parade of Runyan characters: gamblers, chorus girls, a mission band, venders, cops.

Nathan (Sam Levene) gets lovingly touseled by his sweetheart, Adelaide (Vivian Blaine).

Nathan Detroit had troubles, but not with women. For 14 years he had been happily engaged to Adelaide, a hot-spot dancer, and he meant to marry her any minute. His real trouble was that he needed to raise $1000 to rent space in a garage where a crap game could be held in decent seclusion from the cops. To get the cash, he bet handsome Sky Masterson $1000 that he could not entice Sarah, a pure and pretty missionary lass, to Havana. Sky won the bet but he was so overcome by true love he refused to admit his conquest, and decided to cough up the grand.

And so goes *Guys and Dolls*, one of America's best musical comedies, based on a Damon Runyon story. Written by Jo Swirling and Abe Burrows, directed by George Kaufman, and with songs by Frank Loesser, the show brought well-deserved immortality to Runyon's knights of the crap table.

All the gamblers, led by Masterson to Sarah's mission, confess their sins. A prominent sinner is Nicely-Nicely, acted by chubby Stubby Kaye, singing, "Sit down, you're rocking the boat."

Sarah (Isabel Bigley) startles Masterson by getting tipsy and singing, "If I were a bell, I'd be ringing."

Bobby Clark

In this seaside interlude from *As the Girls Go*, Bobby Clark has elected to sit down on a bathing beauty with his arms loftily folded, his eyes gazing imperiously into space. He has created a real whatnot—pleasant to behold, triumphantly above and beyond logic.

The lady beneath the fan is singing a rather famous aria about fairies at the bottom of her garden, as it might be performed by a concert singer with a terrible spate of roguish vivacity. In her long career as the leading female comedian of our time, she has merrily punctured almost every form of human pretense.

Her name is———

Beatrice Lillie

Bibliography

Blum, Daniel. *A Pictorial History of the American Theatre.* New York: Greenberg, 1950.
Blum, Daniel. *Great Stars of the American Stage.* New York: Greenberg, 1952.
Bowers, Faubion. *Japanese Theater.* New York: Hermitage House, 1952.
Cheney, Sheldon. *The Theatre.* New York: Longmans, Green and Company, 1952.
Cleaver, James. *Theatre Through the Ages.* London: George G. Harrap and Company Ltd., 1946.
Dickenson, Thomas S. *The Theatre In A Changing Europe.* New York: Henry Holt and Company, 1937.
Fergusson, Francis. *The Idea of a Theater.* Princeton: Princeton University Press, 1949.
Fitts, Dudley. (Ed.) *Greek Plays In Modern Translation.* New York: Dial Press, 1947.
Freedley, George and John A. Reeves. *History of the Theatre.* New York: Crown Publishers, 1941.
Hamilton, Edith. *The Great Age of Greek Literature.* New York: W. W. Norton and Company Inc., 1942.
Hamilton, Edith. *The Roman Way.* New York: W. W. Norton and Company Inc., 1932.
Hamilton, Clayton. *The Theory of the Theatre.* New York: Henry Holt and Company, 1939.
Harrison, Jane Ellen. *Ancient Art and Ritual.* New York: Henry Holt and Company, 1913.
Hartnoll, Phyllis. (Ed.) *The Oxford Companion to the Theater.* New York: Oxford University Press. 1951.
Hughes, Glenn. *A History of the American Theatre. 1700-1950.* New York: Samuel French, 1951.
Hughes, Glenn. *The Story of the Theatre.* New York: Samuel French, 1928.
Kronenberger, Louis. *Thread of Laughter.* New York: Knopf, 1952.
Laver, James. *DRAMA–Its Costume and Dècor.* New York: The Studio Publications, 1951.
Mantzius, Carl. *A History of Theatrical Art in Ancient and Modern Times.* 6 vols. London: Duckworth, 1906-1921.
Nicoll, Allardyce. *The Development of the Theatre.* New York: Harcourt, Brace and Co., 1937.
Sobel, Bernard. (Ed.) *The Theatre Handbook.* New York: Crown Publishers, 1948.
Stevens, Thomas Wood. *The Theater, from Athens to Broadway.* New York: D. Appleton and Company, 1932.
Stuart, Donald Clive. *The Development of Dramatic Art.* New York: D. Appelton and Company, 1928.

In the introduction to Greek drama the passage from Aeschylus' *Libation Bearers* was taken from *The Great Age of Greek Literature* by Edith Hamilton, W. W. Norton, 1942; the lines from Sophocles' *King Oedipus* and *Oedipus at Colonus* are from *Greek Plays in Modern Translation,* edited by Dudley Fitts, The Dial Press, 1947.

BEATON

BERNAND

BOURKE-WHITE

CAPA

CLARK

COOKE

Photographers

BEATON, CECIL
  Lady Windermere's Fan, 133
  Quadrille, 162
BERNAND, YVETTE
  Trial, The, 116-117
BOURKE-WHITE, MARGARET
  African Ritual, 19 (*top & bottom left*)
BRUGIERE COLLECTION,
N. Y. PUBLIC LIBRARY
  Richard III, 60
CAPA, CORNELL
  Antony and Cleopatra, 145
  Caesar and Cleopatra, 143, 144
  Little Hut, 120-121
  American Indian Ritual, 17
CLARK, ED
  Durante, Jimmy, 226
COOKE, JERRY
  Chinese Theatre, 86-87
CRANE, RALPH
  Fields, W. C., 230
  Marx, Groucho, 230
  Lady Windermere's Fan, 132
CULVER SERVICE
  Hamlet (Barrymore), 72
  Taming of the Shrew, 77
DARBY, EILEEN
  Alice Sit by the Fire, 156-157
  Androcles and the Lion, 137
  Annie Get Your Gun, 238-239
  Carousel, 232-233
  Don Juan in Hell, 148-149 (*bottom*)
  Duchess of Malfi, 80-81
  Frogs, The (*Wellesley College*), 40-41
  (*except bottom p. 41*)
  Henry IV, 62-63
  Henry VIII, 64-65
  Importance of Being Earnest, 134-135
  Man and Superman, 148-149
  (*except top right*)
  Murder in the Cathedral, 52-53
  O Mistress Mine, 163
  Oedipus, 28-29
  On the Town, 236-237
  Playboy of the Western World, 154-155
  Pygmalion, 150-151
  Respectful Prostitute, 114-115
  Savo, Jimmy, 231
  Tempest, The, 66-67 (*bottom*)
  What Every Woman Knows, 158-159
  Would Be Gentleman, 92-93
DAVIS, MYRON
  Porgy and Bess, 210-211
EISENSTAEDT, ALFRED
  Come Back, Little Sheba, 205
  Kabuki Theatre, 88, 89, 90
  Male Animal, The, 208
ELISOFON, ELIOT
  Amphitryon, 45
  Hamlet (Barrault), 73
  Member of the Wedding, 202-203
  Millionairess, The, 140
  Native Son, 184-185
  African Ritual, 18
  Streetcar Named Desire, 197
EYERMAN, J. R.
  School for Scandal, 131
FARBMAN, NAT
  Bacchi, 38-39
  Folies Bergere, 225 (*with McAvoy*)
  Persians, 26-27
FAURER, L.
  Bali Ritual, 21
GARBER, MURRAY
  Love's Labour's Lost, 71 (*bottom left*)
GERARD, EDMUND
  Cherry Orchard, 98-99
  Othello, 75

CRANE

DARBY

DAVIS

EISENSTAEDT

ELISOFON

EYERMAN

FARBMAN

FAURER

GARBER

GERARD

GLINN

GOLDBY

GRANT

GREENE

HALSMAN

HAAS

JOEL

KARGER

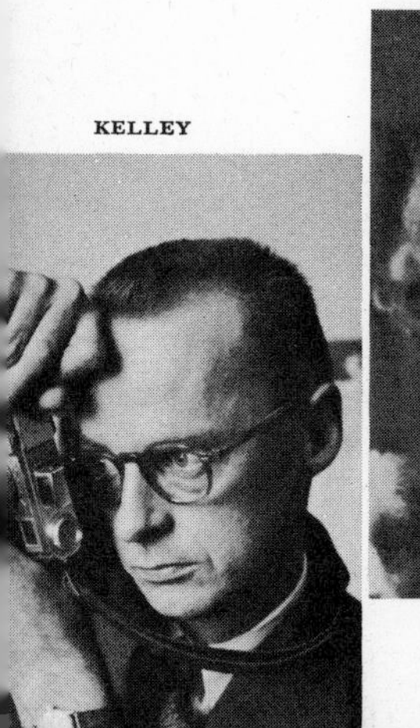
KELLEY

LEEN

McAVOY

McBEAN

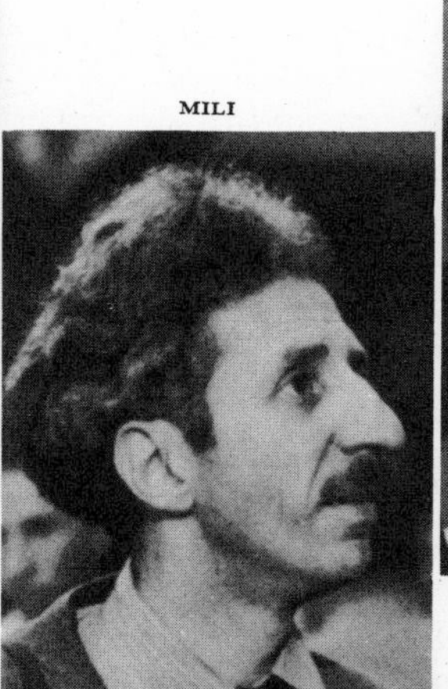
MILI

MORSE

MYDANS

NEWMAN

PARKS

PRESTON

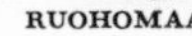

RUOHOMAA

SANDERS

SCHAAL

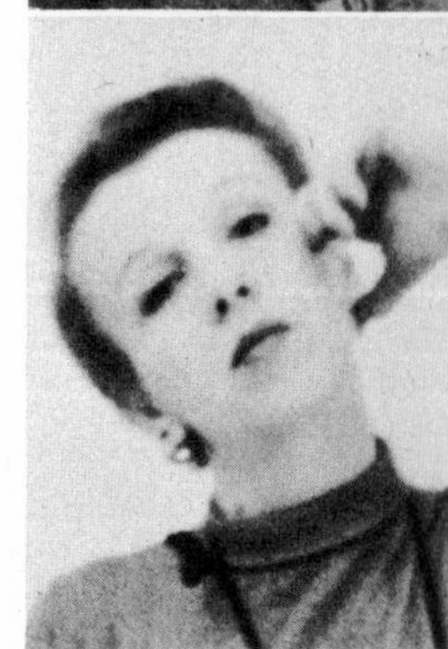

SCHERSCHEL

SHARLAND

SMITH

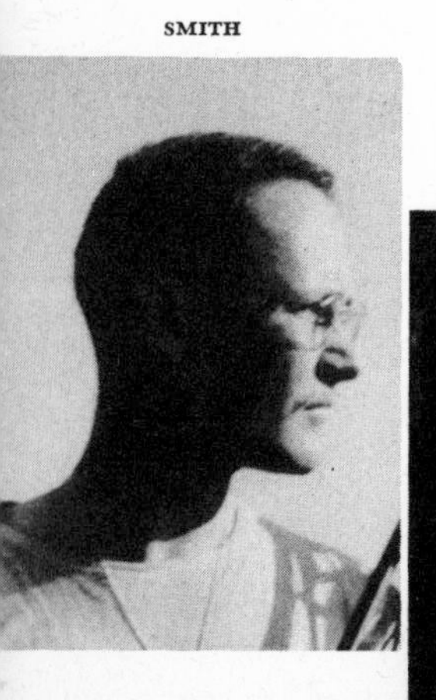

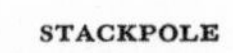

STACKPOLE

STEICHEN

SWOPE

WILD

WOOD

Index